Cincinnati,
City of Seven Hills
and
Five Inclines

By

John H. White, Jr.

Published By

The Cincinnati Railroad Club, Inc.

October 2001

To
Dr. John Stewart M.D.
Best wishes
John H. White Jr.

Cincinnati, City of Seven Hills and Five Inclines

PUBLISHER:

CINCINNATI RAILROAD CLUB, INC.

P. O. BOX 14157

CINCINNATI OHIO 45250-0157

AUTHOR:

John H. White, Jr.

DESIGNERS:

Patrick T. Rose

Linda C. Rose

EDITORIAL STAFF:

James R. Edmonston

Roy F. Hord

Donald Patrick

Robert J. White

Gibson R. Yungblut

This book was published under the direction of the
Publications Committee of the Cincinnati Railroad Club, Inc.

ISBN #

0-9676125-1-9

PRINTED BY:

The Merten Printing Company
a Division of Champion Industries, Inc.
Cincinnati, Ohio

Dedication

In Memory of
John Paul Jones
A life-long transit official and a lover of history
who died March 30, 1984, at the age of 67.

Table of Contents

Acknowledgements

The Cincinnati Railroad Club would like to thank Mr. White for donating the material for this book and especially for donating the proceeds of its sale to the Club.

The Publications Committee would like to extend its heartfelt appreciation to Mr. White for his many hours of cooperation in assembling this work. It was a pleasure to work with an individual so adept and knowledgeable on the subject matter and on the history of Cincinnati in general.

We would also like to thank Mr. Patrick Rose for his many hours of design and lay-out for this volume.

Mr. Donald Patrick served as our initial editor and gave valuable assistance in the editing of the final volume. Other editors included Roy Hord, Jim Edmonston, and Gib Yungblut, to whom no less thanks are owed.

In addition, we would like to acknowledge the Cincinnati Historical Society and the Ohio Historical Society for their cooperation in the reproduction of several of the articles contained herein.

Thanks also to Merten Printing for their help, guidance and participation in this book.

Lastly, we wish to thank President William J. Davis and the Board of Trustees of the Cincinnati Railroad Club, Inc. for their support of this effort.

Linda C. Rose, Chairperson
Publications Committee
Cincinnati Railroad Club, Inc.

Introduction

This book is about the early history of city transit in Cincinnati. It is not, however, a complete or comprehensive study of the subject. It is selective in nature and covers only some aspects of the broad and fascinating story of how our ancestors traveled in and around the Queen City a century or more ago. I do feel, however, that these pages incorporate about as complete a chronicle as can be found in print of the several inclined railways of the region. Because the first chapters are reprints of earlier articles, some details are repeated but all of the text has been updated and expanded. The final chapter is a new and never before published text.

The flight to the suburbs is usually explained as a phenomenon generated by the automobile, but long before the first horseless carriage sputtered over the streets, locals sought ways to escape the smoke, noise and crowded conditions of the city. The very rich removed to the elegant mansions of Mt. Auburn and Clifton. They could commute into town in the luxury of a chauffer driven carriage. The several mainline steam railroads also catered to affluent commuters who rode to suburban villages such as Glendale, Mt. Healthy and Mt. Airy, to all who sought refuge from epidemics that periodically swept Cincinnati.

Around 1875 the middle class found economical transit out of the basin as well. A series of incline railways, horsecar lines and narrow gauge railways offered easy access to the hilltop communities. Transit operators not only laid down tracks, but also put housing and commercial blocks on land that had formerly been home to rows of corn and beans. In this era of rapid technical progress, the horsecars and narrow gauge lines were replaced by efficient electric streetcars starting in 1890. The city remained home to business, the mercantile trade and industry. A few eccentric or stubborn millionaires clung to their old-fashioned townhouses. As always, the poorest classes remained loyal tenants of the least fashionable precincts.

First novels are often thinly disguised autobiographies of the novelist. In a similar fashion, this series of histories was generated by my childhood experiences. A few trips on the Mt. Adams incline made a profound impression on at least one pre-teen youngster that has really never worn off. While the other youngsters collected baseball cards, I searched for newspaper stories and postcards relating to my favorite subject. As a high school student I learned my way around the public library and the historical society. I ventured out to the Western Hills Press to see what their files had to reveal about the Cincinnati and Westwood. I became a visitor at the Street Railway's spacious offices in the Dixie Terminal. Many years before, my grandfather was claim agent for the Traction Company and so I was welcomed, by some colleagues, as Rob Seebaum's grandson. In this way I met Walter Draper, by then retired President of the Cincinnati Street Railway, yet as interested as ever in civic, business and history matters of the area. One of the younger staff members on the property was John Paul Jones, who would one day head Cincinnati Transit and go on to be an executive in the Urban Mass Transit Agency. Paul, as it happened, also had a keen interest in history and was active in the Cincinnati Historical Society for many years. We conspired to save the early records of the local transit industry, which are now held by the Cincinnati Historical Society. Hudson Biery, the Public Relations Director of the Cincinnati Street Railway, patiently dealt with my occasional visits and kindly furnished information of an antiquarian nature. But of all the busy people at the street railway, I must thank Miss Caroline Hein, the long time Secretary of the corporation, most profoundly for her helpfulness. She seemed to enjoy talking about the old times at the traction company, when giants such as W. Kelsey Schoepf and Joseph B. Foraker were running the shop. Back then people listened to words of these powerful leaders. The Traction Company was a major business in the early days of the century. Most people traveled by trolley, it was a big employer, and it had power. When we sat in her office, back in the early 1950's, transit was a declining industry and people who ran it were accordingly diminished. What a strange pair we must have seemed – she a dignified older woman of some position and me, a skinny, feckless, high school student of no station whatever. However, I knew just enough of the history Miss Hein had lived through to make intelligent responses and ask sensible questions. To her mind, I was no doubt young and untutored but not exactly hopeless.

More research was done elsewhere that included a reading of early Cincinnati newspapers. After several years of intermittent work, a small manuscript was produced, which was published in 1957 by the Historical and Philosophical Society of Ohio, predecessor of the Cincinnati Historical Society. This first article lead to many more on a variety of historic subjects. Those pertaining to the local scene have been gathered together for the present volume. A second volume featuring other local railways will appear in about a year.

It is a pleasure to thank the many individuals who helped in the preparation of this book. First, thanks must go to the Cincinnati Railroad Club for sponsoring this volume. Of equal importance were the volunteer efforts of Linda and Patrick Rose for the book's production and layout. Others who helped in so many ways were: Earl W. Clark, Laura Chase, A.S. Eggerton, C.W. Hauck, Dan Finfrock, James W. O'Dell, Jr., Christopher Duckworth, H.A Pence, R.W. Parry, R.C. Post, R.J. White and William Worthington.

I attempted to thank several friends and acquaintances no longer living in the introduction for their help long years ago. To that list I should add Mrs. Alice P. Hook and Vernon Welker.

John H. White, Jr.
Oxford, Ohio
August, 2001

Chapter 1

FROM TOP TO BOTTOM: CINCINNATI'S INCLINES AND HILLTOP HOUSES

Cincinnati is a city of peaks and valleys that claims, like ancient Rome, no fewer than seven hills. The rugged landscape made its setting more picturesque than that of the typical, dead-flat midwestern town. Yet the amphitheater of surrounding hills confined the city to a crescent-shaped basin fronted on the south by the Ohio River. The basin, roughly two miles by one and one-half miles in extent, was fully developed by about 1870. Factories, warehouses, retail shops, tenements, and elegant townhouses clustered tightly in a dense and often tumultuous mixture of rich and poor, of commercial, industrial, and residential occupants. Citizens of every class sought an escape from the congested and sooty atmosphere of the city. Yet, there was no easy access to the high hills that stood in quasi-Olympian remoteness. Those hardy or rich enough to make it to the top might enjoy the pure breezes and clean air so abundant at the summit. The young and athletic might scale the heights on foot, while the wealthy could make the ascent by private carriage. But most common folks could only look up in frustration until some enterprising fellow devised a way to expand the city into the countryside.

In about 1850, the first feeble effort was made with a horse-drawn omnibus up to Mt. Auburn. A double team of four horses was required to haul a twelve-passenger bus up the steep grades of the hillside streets. Allowing for rest stops for the animals to recover their wind, the trip took about thirty minutes. The fare was high because operating costs were equally steep. The bus sure beat walking, but it was too slow and too costly for most Cincinnatians. A horsecar line, which opened in 1867, traversed the same path, but the rail-aided conveyances proved no more satisfactory than the discredited omnibus.

Something more imaginative was needed to solve the special transit needs of the Queen City. The solution was found upriver, in another burgeoning town with a landscape even more rugged than Cincinnati's. Pittsburgh had opened an inclined-plane railway in 1870, specifically designed to carry commuters from the hilltop suburbs to the river-level city. The idea was hardly new. Incline railways had been around since ancient times, but the application to city transit was novel. It was also extremely simple. Two steam engines with large windlasses were placed at the summit. A pair of railroad tracks was built up the hillside to the powerhouse. Steel cables attached to the cars propelled them up and down the track, or plane. The cars ran in opposite directions, as one came up its mate went down. The cars were also counterbalanced by a secondary cable looped around a giant pulley wheel placed inside the powerhouse. In this way, the steam engines rarely had much of a load to move, unless one car was greatly overburdened. The common cable also worked as a safety device in the event one of the hoisting cables should fail.

So here was a ready-made solution, awaiting the chance visit of Joseph Stacy Hill, a Cincinnati soap-maker. Hill was immediately struck by the notion of a hillside elevator as the very thing needed at home. Why hadn't anyone thought of it before? He confided his find to an associate, George A. Smith. Smith had made his fortune building bridges and had an engineering turn of mind. Now involved in real estate development and horsecar lines, he knew that there was good money in public transit, particularly if you were smart enough to buy up land in the destination area before the line opened. Building an inclined-plane railway presented no great technical problem. As for capital, Smith put up most of the money himself. Hill and a few other friends took up the remaining shares of the Cincinnati Inclined Plane Railway Company, which was organized under a state charter in April 1871. The plane would run from the foot of Main Street to the top of Mt. Auburn.

Cincinnati's first incline climbed the slope of Mt. Auburn and opened in 1872. That autumn the Lookout House, seen on the upper left, opened its doors to fun seekers. When the industrial haze intermittently cleared, riders gained a spectacular view of the city. The roof of the lower waiting station is seen in the foreground of this photo. *Cincinnati Historical Society.*

By December of that year, construction was underway on the first of Cincinnati's five inclines. Cooper and Company of Mt. Vernon, Ohio, made the hefty winding machinery, including the two massive iron winding drums. The drums each measured nine feet in diameter by twelve feet wide. Construction problems plus several property-owner lawsuits delayed the opening by a few months. A large crowd attended the May 12, 1872 opening. About six thousand people rode the new incline, without accident or incident, on opening day. Telegraphic signal bells linked the engineer at the top of the hill with the attendants at the bottom station. Passengers were elevated 275 feet in just ninety seconds – now, at last, basin-bound residents had found a fast way out of the city. The incline was seen as a grand success that would change the character of Cincinnati. Henceforth, citizens would view the filthy city as a place fit only for commerce and industry. Their future homes would be out on the hills. Such optimism was not entirely misplaced, for during its first year of operation, the Main Street Incline carried nearly one

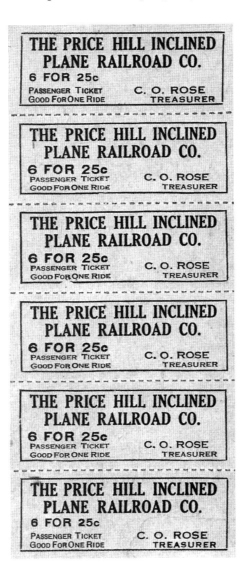

Unlike other Cincinnati inclines, Price Hill featured a second set of tracks, minus the fancy passenger depot at it's foot, for freight wagons. *Cincinnati Historical Society. Tickets courtesy the George T. McDuffie Collection.*

The national economy had slumped into the worst depression in its history following the failure of Jay Cooke and Company in September 1873. Venture capital was difficult to come by, and most would-be incline builders stood pat until the panic subsided. William Price was somewhat less inhibited by the hard times, for he was able to raise money the old-fashioned way - he borrowed it from his father. General Rees E. Price had made a fortune from real estate investments in the city's West End and through the large-scale manufacture of bricks. The younger Price wanted to develop lots on the

Inclines did not require balanced loads in order to function properly. The two open trucks of the Elm Street Incline are shown here about midway passing over Clifton Avenue (now East Clifton). In the distance, directly beyond the upper truck, is the Fairview Incline head-house (see arrow).

highlands of Price Hill, but he needed a transit system to maximize returns. Construction on the Price Hill Incline began in the autumn of 1874. With a grade of 44.6 percent, it would be the steepest of all Cincinnati's inclines. The grand opening came on July 14, 1875 with a crowd so large that the attendants stopped asking for invitations and simply opened the gates to all. The two incline cars were named "Highland Mary" and "Lilly of the Valley" in honor of William's sisters. The Price Hill company opened a parallel incline for freight and wagon traffic in May 1877.

million passengers. Canny George Smith recovered a large portion of his investment during the railway's first season.

Success normally begets hasty imitation. Indeed, a company was founded to build an incline up Price Hill just months after the Main Street plane opened, and, about a year after that, a group incorporated to throw rails up Mt. Adams's craggy slope. Yet, there was no immediate follow-through.

Far to the east of Price Hill stood Mt. Adams, once

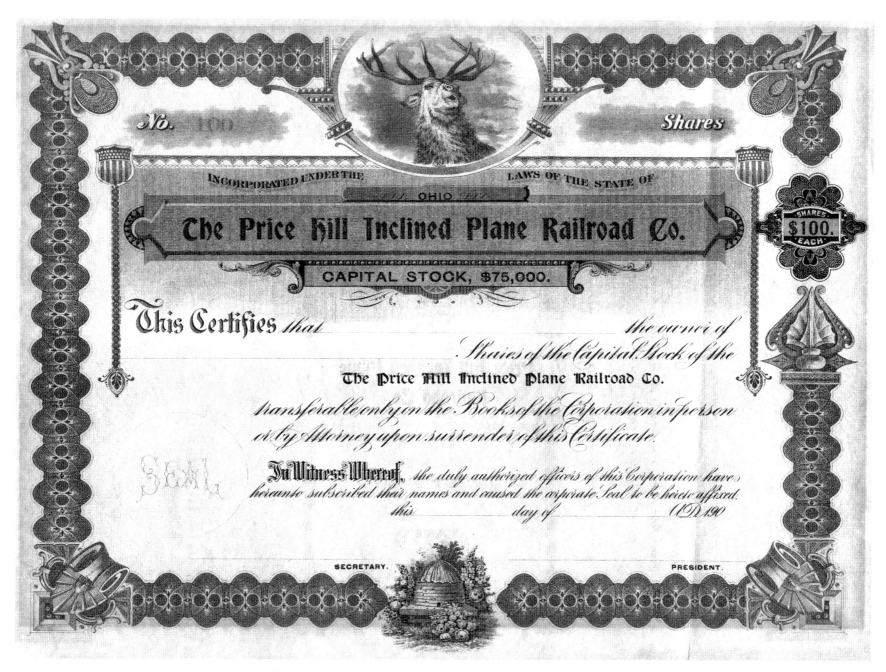

No. 100

Shares

INCORPORATED UNDER THE LAWS OF THE STATE OF

OHIO

The Price Hill Inclined Plane Railroad Co.

CAPITAL STOCK, $75,000.

SHARES $100. EACH

This Certifies that _____ the owner of

_____ Shares of the Capital Stock of the

The Price Hill Inclined Plane Railroad Co.

transferable only on the Books of the Corporation in person or by Attorney upon surrender of this Certificate.

In Witness Whereof, the duly authorized officers of this Corporation have hereunto subscribed their names and caused the corporate Seal to be hereto affixed. this _____ day of _____ A.D. 190

SECRETARY.

PRESIDENT.

Most stock was owned by the McDuffie family, in-laws of the Price family. This unsold share is in the collection of the author.

The Mt. Adams Incline was perhaps the city's best engineered. By 1906, about the time of this photograph, the Highland House site was occupied by the Sterling Glass Works. Rookwood Pottery, on the crest to the left of the head house, is now a restaurant. *Detroit Publishing Company*

home to the Cincinnati Observatory until the smoke and grime of the factories drove it to a more rural setting. The land just behind the brow of the hill was developed into a major park, starting in 1870. Eden Park, because of its elevated remoteness, was inaccessible to the very people it was intended to serve. Construction of an incline began in 1873 but slowed, and then stopped, when funds ran out. After a year or so in limbo, the project seemed dead until one of the original investors provided new capital and hired an energetic promoter named George B. Kerper.

Even Kerper had trouble accelerating the slow march of the trestle and track from Lock Street up the slope to Celestial Street. Finally, on March 8, 1876, the Mt. Adams and Eden Park Inclined Plane Railway opened to the public. At the time it was considered the most finished and best-engineered incline in the area. The two cars were named for pioneer businessmen, Martin Baum and Nicholas Longworth. Some years before, Longworth had operated a vineyard on the very hillside now traversed by the rumbling incline. He had also owned the land occupied by Eden Park, which he referred to

When the Fairview Heights Incline was declared unsafe for street-cars in 1921, car bodies were mounted on the trucks. Commuters had to transfer from streetcar to incline and back again, an unpopular arrangement.

as the Garden of Eden.

Just a few months after the Mt. Adams opening, a fourth incline was finished at the head of Elm Street. It was farthest back from the river and almost at the centerline of the downtown basin. The Cincinnati and Clifton Inclined Plane Railroad Company was incorporated in June 1875 by three well-to-do pork packers. This group moved more quickly than the Mt. Adams people and was ready to open in early September of the following year. At 980 feet, theirs was the longest of the inclines. It was also the most unstable, for the hillside was prone to periodic earth slides, and was routinely rebuilt.

The incline era was nearing its end when Cincinnati's fifth and final plane was built. The Fairview Incline, which did not open until 1894 and was built just around the corner from the Elm Street plane, connected McMicken Street in the basin with Fairview Avenue on the hilltop. The incline faced west and was more or less in line with the present Western Hills Viaduct. The whole thing was done on the cheap with second-hand machinery salvaged from the 1892 rebuilding of the Elm Street Incline. The Fairview plane was built by the Cincinnati Street Railway, which by this date had come to dominate the local transit business. Fairview was built not so much to serve the modest hilltop community surrounding the head-house, but to offer transit to and from the Millcreek Valley for the cross-town streetcar line.

Long before the last incline was opened, street-railway managers understood the need to integrate the inclines into the local transit network, which required direct horsecar lines between the city center and the base station. Conversely, convenient routes radiating out into the hilltop suburbs from the top station had to be developed posthaste. In most cases, while the inclines themselves were under construction, a network of connecting street railways was being developed. The organizers of the Main Street Incline took over the old horsecar line for its downtown connection, but they were forced to construct new lines in the highlands. By 1877, some five years after the incline opened, they reached the zoo. Now it was possible for the denizens of the inner city to view the denizens of the jungle — which needed the bars for protection remained in question. The Elm Street Incline people built a three-mile-long horsecar line out to the city's second largest park, Burnet Woods, about the same time the zoo route opened. Yet, no one could top the scenic route of the Mt. Adams Company that ran the length of Eden Park. The tracks threaded their way through woodlands and grassy hillsides. The cars went past flowerbeds, the art museum, and a handsome lake that actually was a city reservoir. By the late 1880's, the Mt. Adams Company had several connecting lines running more than sixteen miles of track. The operation was profitable as well, for it netted $90,500 in 1888.

Street-railway managers always strove to increase their profits, and one way to accomplish this was to increase ridership. Most traffic met real transportation needs, but owners also could inflate patronage through artificial means. Starting around 1890, some street railways built amusement parks at the end of the line. The incline managers were somewhat ahead of their time in opening resorts adjacent to their upper stations. Food, beer, music, and games were offered at a price, but the greatest attraction was free. The panorama of the city and great river curving past it offered a magnificent bird's-eye view. An escape from the sultry basin during the summer's heat was a special bonus offered to all visitors to any one of the four hilltop resorts. The Main Street Incline's owners opened the Lookout House, the premier hilltop facility, in September 1872. It was a rather plain, two-story wooden structure, with a large, elevated deck and a flat roof. This boxy pleasure palace was leased to a succession of proprietors; the best known was a former saloonkeeper named Frank Harff, who understood the public's fickleness and the need for new or novel attractions to keep them coming back. Good food, pleasant music, and a splendid view were just not enough of a draw. Staged

Line cut of the Bellevue House when new from *Architectural & Building News*, Nov 5, 1876. James W. McLaughlin, Architect. The orchestra sat on a raised platform in the center of the rotunda.

According to a reporter in 1883, so many German burghers and their families visited the Highland House to enjoy the breeze, refreshments, music and view that it was transformed into a Germanic 'stronghold'. *Leslies' Illustrated Newspaper*, August 7, 1880.

ENTERTAINMENT.

Millers' International Exhibition

AND

GRAIN CONGRESS,

AT THE

HIGHLAND HOUSE,

THURSDAY EVENING, JUNE 3, 1880,

AT 8 O'CLOCK.

SEIDENSTICKER'S BAND.

PROGRAMME.

I.

1. Grand March ....Parlow
2. String Quartett—B Flat ....Mozart

Messrs. Jacob Bloom, Max Bendix, Chas. Baetens and Theo. Hahn.

3. Overture—Maritani ....Wallace
4. Selections—Preciosa..Weber
5. Cornet Solo...Levy

Mr. Ruckel.

II.

6. Overture—Pique Dame.......................................Suppe
7. String Quartett— { a Night Song ....Vogt
                     { b Menuett.............................Bocherini
8. Scotch Airs...Bonisson
9. Waltz—Wiener Kinder.......................................Strauss

III.

10. Overture—One Day and One Night in Berlin ....Suppe
11. String Quartett ....Hayden
12. Cornet Solo..Hartman
13. Potpourri—Martha...Flotow
14. Finale ....Strauss

Porter & Williams, Printers, Hopkins' Music Hall, 169 W. Fourth St., Cin.

From an advertising card

HIGHLAND HOUSE

MOUNT ADAMS.

—

GRAND OPENING

—ON—

Thursday Night, December 21,

—WITH—

CURRIER'S CELEBRATED REED BAND.

PROGRAMME.

PART I.

1. Grand March, "Le Prophet"..............Meyerbeer
2. Overture, "Die Frau Meisterin"...............Suppe
3. Waltz (the latest), "Upright Life"............Strauss

PART II.

4. Overture, "Maritana".............................Wallace
5. Fantasia (descriptive), "The Prodigal Son".......................................Dawson
   The latest musical novelty, "Instrumentation"...................By C. M. Currier
6. Polka characteristic, "La Gracieuse"........Herde

PART III.

7. Overture, "Brewer of Preston"...............Adam
8. Waltz, "Sounds from the Vienna Woods"..Strauss
9. Bouffe Selection, "Girofle-Girofla"..........Lecocq

PART IV.

10. Quodlibet Populaire...........................Fr. Zikoff
11. Serenade for Flute and Horn.....................Tittl
    Messrs. Heckle and Kuhn.
12. Finale, "Down the Incline"...................S. Hook
    C. M. CURRIER...................Conductor.

This elegant building, located at the head of Mount Adams and Eden Park Incline Railway, will be open to the public on and after this evening.

Its appointments are so complete in every respect for the comfort and convenience of the guests, that it will only have to be seen to be appreciated.

The Beer Hall, Billiard-Room, Bowling Alleys and Restaurant will be in charge of competent attendants, and every attention will be paid to the comfort of visitors.

1t   **B. F. STARR, Proprietor.**

From *The Cincinnati Enquirer*, 1876

The Bellevue House was designed to attract and awe passengers as they ascended the Elm Street Incline. The retaining wall was put up in 1883 after a major hillside slump weakened the incline's foundation. *Cincinnati Historical Society*

events and special attractions were the secret of his success. One week it was the German Military Band, fresh from their appearance at the Centennial Exhibition in Philadelphia. In June 1877, a live white whale was exhibited in a giant tank filled with salt water. Harff also expanded the facility by adding bowling alleys, an enlarged promenade and a theater.

Both the Highland House, (built next to the Mt. Adams Incline,) and the Bellevue House, (adjacent to the Elm Street plane,) were far grander establishments than the pioneer Lookout House. The Highland featured two towers and a mammoth bay window, while the Bellevue had a great octagon, forty feet in diameter, that seemed to hang in mid-air over the steep hillside. These resorts opened in 1876 and both offered entertainments much like those available at the older Lookout House. The Highland provided a trifle more

of culture than its competitors. In 1877 a concert pavilion was built, and noted symphonic conductor Theodore Thomas was engaged for performances of classical music. Most hilltop patrons, however, were more in the mold of merrymakers, and as many as eight thousand flocked to the Highland on a busy night. The Bellevue House managers considered any day in which one hundred kegs of beer were tapped a good one.

Far around to the west stood the pristine slope of Price Hill, sometimes known as Buttermilk Mountain, because its resort sold no beer or ardent spirits. This policy went back to the enterprise's financial backer, General Price, whose literal reading of the Bible precluded not only alcohol but also apples — the latter being, of course, the forbidden fruit. Price Hill hosts eventually added beer to the bill of fare, but the house maintained its reputation for family-style entertainment. Price Hill House burned in 1899, but the garden restaurant remained open until 1938.

In most cases the inclines outlasted their hilltop resorts by several decades. During their long years of service, most were rebuilt or altered at least once. Mt. Adams, first built with fixed cabs and rather light hoisting machinery, underwent a major reconstruction in 1880, when open platforms and heavier machinery made it possible to receive and lift street vehicles, avoiding the tedious and time-consuming transfer of passengers between horsecars and incline cars. The horsecar simply rolled onto a platform and was taken up or down the plane. The Main Street Incline underwent a similar reconstruction after a frightful accident in 1889 that killed six passengers. The new machinery and open platforms did not fully reassure the traveling public, and Main Street was abandoned in 1898. Elm Street was twice reconstructed, in 1890 and 1892. Not only were open platforms and more substantial machinery added, but also a portion of the trestle was made of steel rather than wood.

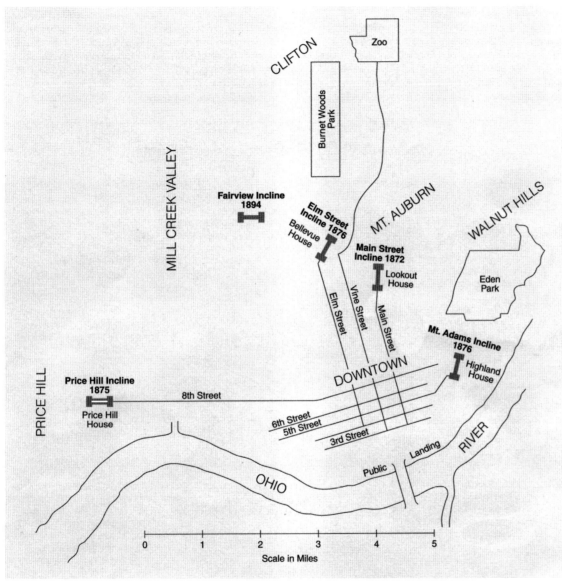

The City of Seven Hills and Five Inclines.

been an open-platform operation. The Price Hill Company did modernize in 1928 by replacing its steam power plant with an electric motor. All the other inclines in Cincinnati remained steam powered until the end.

As do so many good things, the inclines outlived their usefulness. By 1900 the Traction Company viewed them as traffic bottlenecks, particularly at rush hour. Loading, unloading, and the trip up and down simply took too long. The fastest rate at which cars could be handled was one every 3 1/2 minutes. Still, all but the Main Street plane survived well into the twentieth century. Daily riders saw them as anything but obsolete, and unwilling to alienate the traveling public, the Traction Company reluctantly continued operations. And then a rather backhanded tactic was used to get rid of one. In June 1926 the Elm Street Incline was closed for "repairs". The renovation just never seemed to get under way — in fact, a long-term dismantling took place, ending in 1949, when the powerhouse was at last razed. Things moved a little quicker at Fairview, which was shut down late in 1923. While local residents negotiated for a reopening with the Traction Company, a mysterious fire leveled the powerhouse, so ending any hope of restored service.

Price Hill continued on as a moderately profitable family enterprise. The realities of urban transit eventually

The Price Hill Incline remained independent of the street-railway monopoly and retained the old-fashioned, fixed cabs for passenger service. The adjacent freight carrier had always

Cincinnati's inclines suffered only two accidents of any consequence during more than seven decades of operation. One occurred at the Price Hill Incline in the autumn of 1906, when a cable on the freight tracks snapped just before the truck, carrying two wagons, reached the top. The safety cable slowed but did not stop the rapid descent. Although the two teamsters escaped without serious injury, the horses had to be destroyed.
Cincinnati Historical Society

Arched iron bridges carried this incline, the city's steepest, over two city streets in it's ascent of Price Hill. The photograph above was taken in the early 20th century.
Cincinnati Historical Society

The machinery that operated an inclined plane was housed in the basement of the head-house. A single safety cable and two hoisting cables ran between the two platforms. Steam engines (the crank of one of the Mt. Adams engines is seen in the foreground of the photo at right) in the incline's head-house powered two winding drums for the cables. These cables controlled the platforms, or trucks, carrying passengers and freight. The two drums operated in opposite directions so that as one truck went up, the other went down.

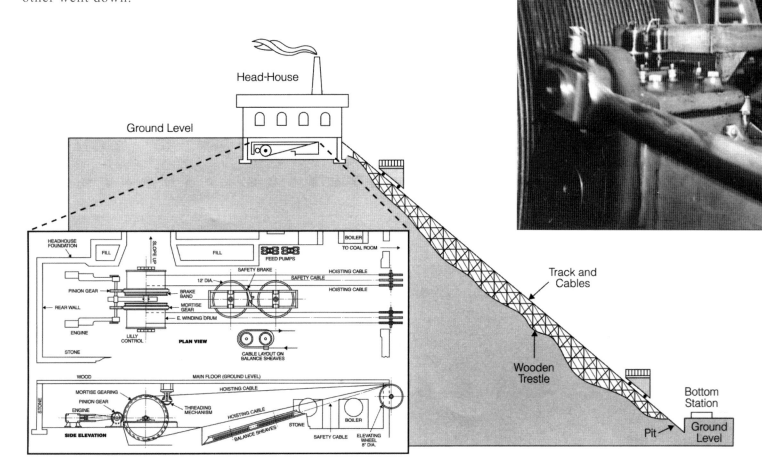

Head-House

Ground Level

HEADHOUSE FOUNDATION
FILL
SLOPE UP
FILL
BOILER
TO COAL ROOM
FEED PUMPS

SAFETY BRAKE
HOISTING CABLE
SAFETY CABLE
12' DIA.
HOISTING CABLE
PINION GEAR
BRAKE BAND
MORTISE GEAR
REAR WALL
E. WINDING DRUM
ENGINE
LILLY CONTROL
PLAN VIEW
STONE
CABLE LAYOUT ON BALANCE SHEAVES

WOOD
MAIN FLOOR (GROUND LEVEL)
MORTISE GEARING
HOISTING CABLE
PINION GEAR
THREADING MECHANISM
ENGINE
STONE
HOISTING CABLE
SIDE ELEVATION
BALANCE SHEAVES
STONE
BOILER
SAFETY CABLE
ELEVATING WHEEL 8' DIA.

Track and Cables

Wooden Trestle

Bottom Station

Pit
Ground Level

overran this mom-and-pop operation, as more and more commuters went by automobile or the faster trolleys that bypassed the incline. Only those living in the immediate vicinity of the incline found it very convenient. The freight plane closed down in 1929 as motor trucks replaced horse-drawn wagons. Meanwhile, the passenger count slipped. The Great Depression brought corner cutting on maintenance expenditures. In July 1943 a minor derailment led to an inspection that revealed the entire trestle was rotten. During a long debate in which all of the principals (including the city government) denied responsibility, the incline remained idle before being dismantled in 1947.

This left Mt. Adams as the city's last incline. It too, was threatened by high operating costs, a declining traffic, and maintenance headaches. The obsolete machinery was in need of replacement, or at least modernization. The street railway company's traffic and revenues were in perilous decline, and the thought of pouring money into a museum-style operation dear only to the tourist board seemed foolish. If the incline was so important, let the city take it over. The city wanted it, but did not want to pay for it. Could the county run it? Or perhaps the state or maybe some wealthy, private benefactor would come through? This airy sort of talk went for several years, and like most such talk, it achieved nothing more than heavy newspaper coverage. Meanwhile, back on terra firma, a field inspection of the trestle revealed many weaknesses. The incline was declared a hazard and was accordingly closed. The final day of operation was April 16, 1948.

Today, the site of the Mt. Adams Incline is a parking lot filled with shiny automobiles. Some twenty feet below the asphalt are the moldering foundations of the hoisting machinery. Nothing here imparts a sense of the once-great public facility that stood on the brow of Mt. Adams. On the right is the old Rookwood Pottery, now housing a restaurant.

And to the left is a nondescript apartment building where the Highland House once stood. One must look carefully to find any vestige of the old order. Down the hillside, among the weeds and trash trees, one can still see the crumbled stone piers of the inclined-plane structure. Little else remains to memorialize Cincinnati's incline era.

AN INCLINE RECOLLECTION

Between the ages of seven and twelve, my brother and I would spend a week or two with my grandmother in East Walnut Hills so my parents might have a little vacation time away from the kids. These visits were generally a quiet time for two active boys, for Grandmother naturally lived a quiet life. But, she would try to liven things up a little by cooking up a batch of fresh donuts — on the basement laundry stove so as not to grease up the kitchen; or she would pull out the Chinese checkers or some other game after dinner.

Yet, to me, the highlight of the visit was always our shopping excursion downtown. My grandmother had no pension or Social Security, but lived on the savings of her late husband. That meant she had to count her pennies. Once a week, she would head downtown to the Findlay or Central Markets to load up on potatoes, lard, cabbage, sausage, and whatever else looked good. She was convinced the market food was not only cheaper, but also fresher than anything she could find in the grocery.

Off she would go with four or five knit shopping bags, on foot, five blocks down Hewitt Avenue to Montgomery Road. At this point, we could board a streetcar heading for downtown via Gilbert Avenue. This was the simple and direct way to go, but I always pleaded to take the Zoo-Eden car. This meant a transfer — more time and trouble than it was worth to my grandmother but a major priority to me, because the Zoo-Eden line went into the city via the Mt. Adams Incline. Now wasn't that worth a little extra time and trouble — oh, come on, Grandma —here comes a Number 4 that will take us right to Peebles Corner where we can get one of the zoo cars. Sometimes the wait at Peebles got a little long because the Zoo-Eden wasn't such a popular line.

Once aboard, I was happy. We would roll down Gilbert Avenue for a few blocks, swing off to a side street, and then pop out into Eden Park on a private track — just like a real railroad. This would lead us over the spindly Eden Park entrance bridge, then back into the woods, past the Art Museum and back onto the streets of Mt. Adams. Ahead was the head-house of the Mt. Adams Incline. The heavy orange and cream colored streetcar slowed down as if it were approaching a dangerous abyss. We bumped over a couple of rough switches and rolled cautiously onto the left-hand track. We stopped fully, and then our car crept forward ever so slowly onto the waiting incline platform. There was the city before us.

I felt we were a thousand feet above everything and that some playful God had created a miniature Cincinnati just for me. Then my fanciful thoughts were interrupted by the clang of the

One wonders what today's safety regulators would say about permitting passengers, especially children, to stand outside the trolley car on the Mt. Adams Incline. *Earl Clark photo.*

iron gate at the back of the platform and the streetcar motorman winding up the big hand brake in the front of the car. "Let's go outside," my brother said. Grandmother stayed in her seat — she would need her strength for the marketing. My brother and I stepped down out of the streetcar, onto the platform. There was a faint tinkling of signal bells. We were moving very slowly at first, but wow! did we pick up speed fast. Had the cables let loose? But, no, they were obediently trailing behind as some forty tons of steel rolled down, down, down at a pace too fast for my nervous, young stomach. At midpoint we passed the upward bound platform and car. The city seemed to be rushing upward to meet us. And then the descent smoothly slackened as the bottom station came into view. This wonderful roller-coaster-like ride was over in about ninety seconds. My brother and I scurried back aboard and were quickly seated next to our indulgent grandmother. The streetcar roughly ground its way off of the platform and onto the tracks buried in Lock Street. Our Incline ride was over, but my memory of those few rides will remain as fresh and real as the azaleas in my front garden.

Chapter 2

THE CINCINNATI INCLINED PLANE RAILWAY COMPANY: THE MOUNT AUBURN INCLINE AND THE LOOKOUT HOUSE

Jackson Park, one of the most inaccessible parcels of public land in Cincinnati, is situated at the end of a labyrinth of dead-end streets just east of Christ Hospital in Mount Auburn. Despite its forbidding approach, this obscure neck of land rising high above the city witnessed the beginnings of suburban public transit in Cincinnati. The city's first incline and earliest electric street railway of any length started at this location.

Although a few suburban villages far from the urban center had been established early in the city's development, Mount Auburn was one of the first close-in hilltop communities to be settled. The lofty eminence of Jackson Hill, which removed it from the bustle and confusion of the basin made it a desirable residential area. By the 1850's, a female seminary, Mount Auburn Young Ladies Institute, was in operation, broad avenues were graded, and the landscape was dotted with handsome estates. It was a rich man's community from which the residents could afford private conveyance to the city, but there were some who desired the convenience and economy of public transit. This need was answered about 1850 by the establishment of an omnibus line. The horse-drawn bus was never satisfactory, however; it was slow, expensive, and often "crowded to suffocation inside with passengers of both sexes and 'many minds'...." [1] The trip from the center of the city took nearly two hours,

the most grueling portion of which was the ascent up Sycamore Street Hill. Even though a double team was used, a heavily-loaded bus necessitated several stops to rest the exhausted horses. During winter months, if Sycamore Hill was icy; service was suspended entirely. In addition, the fifteen-to-twenty cent fare was thought exorbitant at the time.

The prospects for improved transit grew brighter in 1864 when the Mount Auburn Street Railroad was organized. Chartered as Route 8, this company planned to build a line from Fifth and Main Streets to Auburn Avenue. The difficulties of surmounting Jackson Hill were recognized in the liberal provisions of the franchise, which permitted the contractor to select whatever streets offered the easiest grade so long as a majority of the homeowners along the way did not object. Progress was very slow, possibly due to a shortage of materials and labor during the Civil War. By April 1867, the tracks reached the foot of Jackson Hill at Orchard Street, and by late June cars were running to the top of the hill. The route was a circuitous one: after the long grade up the eastward slope of Liberty Street, the tracks turned north on Highland, then west on Ringgold, north on Josephine, and finally on to Auburn Avenue. Again a double team was necessary, with all the attendant annoyances and delays involved in hitching and unhitching the extra horses. The Mount Auburn railway offered little improvement over the omnibus. The trip was nearly as slow and the small, cramped bobtail cars were no more comfortable. Meager patronage led to indifferent maintenance of the tracks, resulting in

[1] *Cincinnati Gazette*, June 25, 1872, gives an amusing account of the Mount Auburn omnibus. Other facts on this subject were found in the Gazette, April 29, 1871, and the Scientific American, February 22, 1873, p. 116.

frequent derailments. The Cincinnati Gazette waggishly suggested that old citizens who wished to refresh their memory of the ancient corduroy road need only board a Mount Auburn horsecar.[2]

Meanwhile, a solution to the hilltop transportation problem in Cincinnati was being perfected upriver at Pittsburgh. A giant steam-powered hillside elevator, known more precisely as an inclined plane railway, was opened in the spring of 1870. The Monongahela incline connected the hilltop community of Mount Washington with the city of Pittsburgh. Soon after the incline opened, Joseph Stacy Hill (1813-1893), a Cincinnati soap manufacturer, visited Pittsburgh where he was struck by the obvious application of this scheme to Cincinnati's vertical transit problem.[3] He enthusiastically reported the idea to George A. Smith (1820-1888), who was not only a man of property but also a practical mechanic and an experienced contractor.[4] Smith had built all the piers for the Suspension Bridge connecting Cincinnati and Covington, Kentucky; the railroad bridge between Cincinnati and Newport, Kentucky; and the pontoon bridge across the Ohio River during the Civil War. His interests spanned real estate and public transport as well.

Thus Hill had made his suggestion to a man of energy and means who wasted no time in implementing the plan. Smith in turn called on James M. Doherty to supervise the project. Doherty and Smith had been acquaintances since the mid-1840's when as young men they served as conductors on the Little Miami Railroad. Doherty had worked for Arthur Latham and Company, operators of several Cincinnati omnibus lines, and in more recent years was an official of a

Superintendent James Monroe Doherty

local street railway.[5] The organization papers for a steam railroad, initiated some twenty years earlier but never built, were used to obtain a charter from the Ohio State Legislature on April 21, 1871. In this way the company hoped to be free of regulations and restrictive street railway laws imposed by the city. Despite this somewhat questionable maneuver, it still was necessary to obtain permission from the city for crossing the various lateral streets above Jackson Hill. The necessary ordinance was passed in May 1871, and the

---

[2] *Cincinnati Gazette*, October 30, 1872.

[3] Information on J. S. Hill, Jr. The manuscript is in the collection of The Cincinnati Historical Society.

[4] See various Cincinnati newspapers, January 4, 1888, for obituary notices of Smith.

[5] *Cincinnati: The Queen City of the West*, ed., George Mortimer Roe (The Cincinnati Times Star Co., 1895), p. 268-69.

In 1889 the Cincinnati Incline Plane Railway put into operation the first major electric streetcars in the city. A motorman, William Nagel, stands at the front of the car.

Cincinnati Inclined Plane Railway Company (hereafter referred to as the C.I.P.) was grudgingly recognized. George A. Smith held all but five shares of stock in the company.

By mid-December construction was underway and the equipment was ready for delivery. The machinery consisted of two boilers, a pair of reciprocating steam engines with 12 inch by 24 inch cylinders (70 horsepower), two winding drums 9 feet in diameter by 12 feet in length, and safety wheels and brake mechanisms. Cooper and Company of Mt. Vernon, Ohio, built the engines and winding apparatus. The passenger car bodies were completed by February 1872, and it was hoped the incline would open by the first of March.[6] But the plane was not ready for a test run until April 20, when all was reported ready for opening to the public except for a pending lawsuit in which several property owners along the line had obtained an injunction against the Incline Company. The suit was soon resolved and the grand opening was held on May 12, 1872.

The opening of the first incline in the city was expected to draw a large crowd, but the number of curiosity seekers was swelled by patrons bound for the annual festival of the German Protestant Orphan Home in Mount Auburn. The police were on hand to direct the crowds both at the bottom station at Mulberry and Main Streets, and at the top station on Jackson Hill. An estimated six thousand persons were carried up and down the first day. No mishaps were reported, though the engineer and other crew members were admittedly nervous in running the machinery for the first

time with passengers aboard. An ingenious telegraphic system of signal bells permitted communication between the operating engineer in the powerhouse at the top of the hill and the attendant at the bottom station. Two bells rang for "ready;" one for "alarm," signaling that the doors were closed and locked; and three for "start." The 850-foot trip took 1-1/2 minutes; at last there was a speedy avenue from Mount Auburn to the city. The city papers pronounced the incline not only a grand success but also an invention that would change the character of the city. Henceforth, citizens would leave the crowded, filthy city to commerce and industry, inasmuch as "the future home of the future Cincinnatians will be out on hills..."[7] This prediction was borne out by the four other inclines which opened in subsequent years.[8]

Once the incline was successfully running, the owners of the C.I.P. decided to build a connecting system of horsecar lines. At the bottom, a horse-car line was to be constructed from the station at Mulberry and Main Streets down Main to the Fifth Street Market (Fountain Square) in the center of town. Construction for this line was authorized by the city in December 1871, and rails were on order when the incline opened in 1872, but progress was slow. Smith and his associates gained control of the Mount Auburn Street Railroad in the winter of 1872. The competing Mount Auburn line (Route 8) was absorbed in the take-over, and its tortuous

[6] *Cincinnati Gazette*, February 19, 1872.

[7] *Cincinnati Enquirer*, May 13, 1872.

[8] The other inclines operated in Cincinnati, and their opening dates, were: Price Hill (1875), Mount Adams (1876), Elm Street (1876), Fairview (1894).

Developers of the Lookout House invested relatively little in this resort's architecture, confident that the view itself would draw customers. The fat brick chimney to the right is part of the top station power house - note the incline car at the far right.

Jackson Hill line was abandoned. Temporarily, a spur track was built over to Liberty Street where a connection was made with the Mount Auburn Street Railroad, which conveyed cars of the C.I.P. into the city's center. This branch was opened in April 1873. The new Main Street horsecar line affording a direct route between downtown and the base of the incline at Mulberry and Main Streets was eventually opened on May 16, 1873. [9]

At the same time, work on a horsecar line from the top station to Auburn Avenue was underway. As a temporary measure, within two months of the incline's opening, omnibuses were operating from the top of the incline to the adjacent suburbs of Clifton, Avondale, and Walnut Hills. These connecting lines assured a steady volume of traffic for the incline. By June 1872, six hundred passengers daily were riding the incline; traffic during the first year was reported to be a million persons. [10] The relatively high fare

[9] *Cincinnati Gazette*, May 17, 1873.

[10] *Scientific American Supplement*, April 20, 1878, p. 1905-06.

did not seem to discourage passengers. Twelve combination city-incline tickets sold for one dollar; twenty incline tickets alone cost the same price. When complaints were heard, Superintendent Doherty countered that the old Route 8 failed twice on the five-cent fare. He added that transportation was expensive and the public must expect to pay for it. [11]

It occurred to Smith not long after the incline opened that the magnificent overlook of city and river from the top station made an ideal site for a public garden. If it attractively provided entertainment and refreshment, even plain folk who could not afford to live in Mount Auburn would ride the incline for an evening's amusement. Hopefully, the place would pay for itself and generate excursion traffic for the incline. The idea appeared a sound one and Smith decided to build not only a garden but also a "refreshment saloon" so that year-round operations could be maintained. A crew of carpenters were put to work, and, obviously without the advice of an architect, built a simple two-story wooden building that was little more than a promenade. Plain as a mud scow, it was named the Lookout House and was declared a magnificent pleasure palace when completed in the fall of 1872. It measured 50 by 150 feet, with a 50-foot square kitchen at the rear. [12] The first floor served as the bar and wine room; a dancing hall and smaller refreshment room occupied the upper floor.

Sunday was the busiest day at the Lookout House. The Sunday closing laws were brazenly ignored as beer and wine were sold openly. The noisy crowd became a nuisance to the staid residents of Mount Auburn. One of them wrote a vitriolic condemnation of the low morals tolerated on the Sabbath; the music was of a kind ".. that provokes thirst, and the impatient clinking of beer mugs can be heard on every hand." [13] Despite this and other protests, no official action

LOOKOUT HOUSE   FRANK HARFF.   CINCINNATI, O.
PROPRIETOR.

The artist took some artistic license in depicting this scene. Lookout House is on the left; engine house and incline on the right but the hillside is shortened. An amphitheater was used for dramatic and circus performances.

was taken for another twenty years, when a stricter enforcement of the law closed all of the hilltop houses forever.

The Cincinnati Inclined Plane Railway Company had no interest in managing the Lookout House but instead leased it to an independent operator. George Kemmeter was the first proprietor, followed by Frank Harff, who proved to be an innovator in hilltop house management. A former Vine Street saloonkeeper, Harff saw the need for special attractions to promote greater patronage. Fireworks, bands, and balloon ascensions became the stock-in-trade at the Lookout House. In September 1876, Harff brought the famous German Military Band, then on tour after playing at the United States Centennial Exposition in Philadelphia, to the Lookout House where it played to an audience of ten thousand. The following June, Harff exhibited one of the greatest attractions ever

[11] *Cincinnati Gazette*, July 11, 1873.
[12] Ibid., September 24, 1872.
[13] Ibid., May 21, 1873.

Frank Harff, the dazzling promoter of the Lookout House, ignored Sunday closing laws and established his hilltop attraction as a model which other belvederes later copied. From the *Cincinnati Business Directory* 1887-1888.

shown in the city, a giant white whale.[14] The mammal was transported from the East in a boxcar fitted with a tank. Harff erected an exhibit tank holding 168,000 gallons of water, to which salt was added until a sea-like solution was simulated. But the whale did not thrive in its artificial environment; by early July the public was encouraged to "see it today, for tomorrow it may be dead." When it did die a few days later,

[14] Ibid., June 21, 1877.

its body was embalmed, a process guaranteed for six months. Yet within a day or two a repellent odor began to be remarked by visitors to the Lookout House. The stench soon became so vile that the whale was hastily removed to a soap factory for rendering while the building underwent massive fumigation. All this notoriety created the sensational interest that Harff craved for the Lookout House.

During the years of Harff's management, many improvements were made to the grounds and buildings. He added bowling alleys, enlarged the promenade, and in 1878 erected a theater. Octagonal in shape, its pagoda-like roof added much-needed architectural interest to the Lookout House. Among the plays produced there in the early years were "Our Boarding House," "All That Glitters is Not Gold," and "Uncle Tom's Cabin." Banquets were another important source of business at the Lookout House. In July 1877, the Board of Trade held its grand banquet with a six-course meal that can only be described as Roman. Currier's Orchestra provided entertainment and a Prof. Weiffenback performed solo pieces on sixteen drums. The National Brewers' Congress banquet was also held there.

Frank Harff departed the Lookout House in 1878 to take over management of the Highland House on Mount Adams. The succeeding managers never matched his genius and the other hilltop houses of Cincinnati soon eclipsed the Lookout House. The Lookout House should be remembered, however, as the prototype after which the others were modeled.

In September of 1875 the Zoological Gardens opened, not as a public enterprise but as a privately owned stock company. Among its founders was George A. Smith, who saw obvious traffic potential for his inclined plane. It would only be necessary to extend the tracks up Vine Street from Auburn Avenue to connect the Zoo with a direct line to the city via the incline. A month after the Zoo's opening, the city gave the C.I.P. permission to lay tracks on Vine Street. The C.I.P. in turn

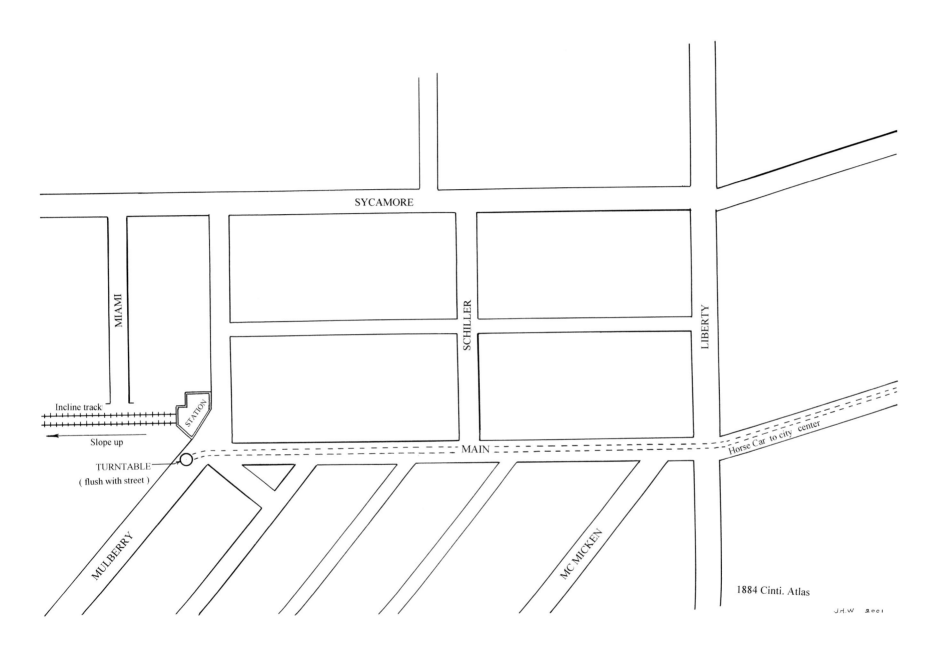

Bottom Station, Cincinnati Incline Plane Railway Company and the surrounding street grid.
From the Sanborn Fire Insurance maps

purchased some shares to ingratiate itself with the Zoo's management. Construction of the new line languished, however, perhaps due to the depression following the Panic of 1873. The Auburn Avenue segment was double-tracked in the spring of 1876, but little work was done on the Vine Street line until the following year. By early August of 1877 the extension was open to Hammond and Vine, a little over a half mile from the Zoo entrance. [15] On September 13 the extension reached the Zoo entrance, the double tracking of Vine Street from Auburn Avenue was completed, and through downtown service was inaugurated. Traffic justified the extension as some three thousand passengers visited the Zoo on a Sunday.

Several weeks after the opening, a steam dummy locomotive from the Baldwin Locomotive Works was obtained for trial on the upper end of the Vine Street line. It ran only 3,300 feet from Hammond Street to the Zoo entrance, horses being used on the remainder of the system. If the dummy proved successful, operation would be extended to the top of the incline, and more "silent steam motors" might be purchased. At least this was the hope of the Baldwin Locomotive Works, which at the time was promoting dummy locomotives for street railways by sending demonstrators across the country for trial. One other horsecar line in Cincinnati wanted to try a dummy but the city council refused to grant even a sixty-day trial. [16] The C.I.P. ignored the city ruling, although its franchise for the Vine Street line specifically stated that only horses or mules might be used for power. The C.I.P. fell back on its state railroad charter, which allowed it to use steam. The dummy proved expensive to operate; wages and fuel came to $8.50 a day, with yearly maintenance and depreciation figured at twenty-five percent of the original construction cost. Little is known of the dummy's operations after late October 1877, but it was presumably returned to the builder for resale.

The next ten years were uneventful ones for the C.I.P. The management was content to operate the small six-mile system. During these years the company owned 24 cars and 145 horses and mules, and employed 90 men. [17] In 1881, 2.3 million passengers were carried; six years later the number of riders was up 600,000. Net earnings averaged $18,000 per year. While the capital stock was authorized at one million dollars, only $10,500 was paid in during the early years, the cost of the company being carried by a $125,000 first mortgage. In 1884 nearly half a million dollars in stock was sold, but since no new tangible assets were acquired the new-investors were surely receiving "blue sky" certificates for their investment. No effort was made to repay the mortgage.

While Smith, Doherty, and Hill were content with things as they were, the residents of Mount Auburn were losing patience with the C.I.P.and its complacent ways. The fare was high: five cents from downtown to the incline, five cents for the incline, and another fare for the connecting car at the top. To save wages young boys were employed as drivers and conductors. Generally rude and insolent, the gang of "street toughs" who operated the cars didn't help to endear the road to those required to travel on it. Though the other street railways of the city were busily building extensions, acquiring new cars, and even adopting cable power for the heavily traveled routes, the C.I.P. indolently drifted along.

While most passengers only grumbled, one decided to build a competing cable railway to spark the C.I.P. into either action or abandonment. Henry Martin had invested heavily in real estate in the area and realized it would never mature in value unless truly satisfactory transit was available. Thus motivated, he organized the Mount Auburn Cable Railway in 1886. The route was to start at Fourth and Sycamore, then proceed up

---

[15] Ibid., August 8, 1877.

[16] Ibid., August 28, 1877, noted the desire of the Walnut Hills line for a trial of steam dummies.

[17] Ohio Railroad Commission Reports, 1880-1887, is the basis for these and the subsequent figures.

Cincinnati Inclined Plane Railway steam dummy #1 operated briefly in 1877.

Monday, so as not to sully himself with operating a business on Sunday . The new cable line cut deeply into the C.I.P.'s traffic. Riders were down nearly fifty percent. Though the net loss for the year was surprisingly small, only $3,500, confidence in the company's future was badly shaken. The stock fell to one cent on the dollar.[18] George Smith's death in January 1888 was the final blow for the C.I.P. The executors of his estate, fearing the company would fail, decided to sell. Smith was virtually the sole owner. Doherty and Hill had only a few shares each and neither had private funds to save the company. Complete abandonment looked imminent.

It was thought that perhaps the Kilgour brothers, Charles and John, owners of the Cincinnati Street Railway Company, would buy up the shares, but apparently they were too involved in developing the lines already in their control and in acquiring George Kerper's lines, a competitive system and the second largest in the city.[19] Possibly they simply hoped the C.I.P. would vanish, allowing their Cincinnati Street Railway Company to step in and take over the lucrative excursion traffic by extending

Sycamore Street Hill, and by various streets go north on Highland and Burnet Avenues to the village of Avondale. Construction proceeded through 1887, but the engineering was second-rate and Martin, inexperienced in street railway matters, made many mistakes. Still, he was a wealthy, strong-willed man who finally saw the first section of the line opened in March 1888. The entire road to Avondale opened in June of that year. Though Martin's management was inept and he himself exhibited eccentricities such as his insistence on selling the line to his superintendent every Saturday and reclaiming the title on

[18] *Street Railway Gazette*, July 1888, p. 95-96.
[19] See chapter 3 of this volume.

its Vine Street cable line to the Zoo. None of this, however, came to pass. In a surprise move a syndicate from Louisville, headed by Hardin H. Littell and backed by Fidelity Trust Company of Louisville, bought a controlling interest in the C.I.P. in the fall of 1888. Littell was an experienced street railway man of national reputation who had started with the Louisville City Railway as a lad of nineteen and become its superintendent three years later.[20] He helped organize the American Street Railway Association and was elected its first president in 1882. His brother, Harvey M. Littell, then managing a line in St. Paul, Minnesota, was brought to Cincinnati to direct the C.I.P. Doherty was retained as secretary out of respect for his long service and experience.

The Littells' realized that a crash modernization program was needed to revitalize the C.I.P. Electric traction had proved practical a few months earlier when Frank J. Sprague's pioneering line in Richmond, Virginia, was opened. While more conservative street railway men would wait a year or two to see a more complete test, the Littells' decided to plunge ahead, and contracted with Sprague in November 1888 to purchase twenty new electric cars. A generating plant was built next to the incline powerhouse, and the incline was rebuilt with open platforms so that the electric cars themselves might be raised or lowered. The old fixed cab incline bodies were removed; with the new system the tedious, time-consuming transfer was eliminated. When the new system was put in service in June 1889, Cincinnati's first electric streetcar line of any consequence was opened.[21]

Some months before the opening, the new management of the C.I.P. had an opportunity to show its aggressive spirit. The Martin cable line had extended its line east from Burnet along Erkenbrecher Avenue to the Zoo's main entrance, thus threatening to take a portion of the traffic since the C.I.P. tracks were somewhat farther from the entrance. The Littells corrected this with a bold countermove: "Working in the mud and under a pouring rain, they extended their tracks from the former Terminus right to the new gates of the Garden."[22] The construction, directly across the property of the Zoo, was done without the knowledge and consent of its trustees. While the action was presumptuous, there is no evidence that the Littells were ever forced to remove the tracks.

The electric cars were operating smoothly, patronage was good, and the Littells were busy with plans for a ten-mile extension to Carthage. A minor accident at the incline on July 14, 1889, resulted in a return to the fixed-cab system, with transfer of passengers at the top and bottom stations. The old winding machinery had been retained and was admittedly too light for trucking streetcars on open platforms. While no serious injuries resulted from the mishap, it foretold of a far grimmer event.

It was Tuesday, October 15, 1889, and the noon bells were ringing.[23] Eight passengers bound home for lunch boarded the incline car for the ascent to Mount Auburn. The trip proceeded normally until the car approached the summit, but instead of slowing down it continued at full speed with a fearful crash into the top station. The engines continued to turn, holding the car at the top of the plane, but with such force that both the hoisting and safety cables were pulled

[20] *Street Railway Review*, February 1891, p. 52.
[21] The Mount Adams & Eden Park Inclined Plane Railway opened a short electric line with Daft motors on Oak Street in April 1889 but it was largely an experimental operation.

[22] Street Railway Journal, February 1889, p. 44.
[23] Accounts of the October 15, 1889, accident were found in the Cincinnati newspapers on October 16 and 17. The coroner's hearing was reported on November 6 of that year.

The tragedy of October 15, 1889 as sketched by a *Cincinnati Enquirer* artist at the time.

flying debris. Who was responsible for this monstrous horror? The coroner's investigation revealed several defects in the machinery: the clips holding the cables were not secure, no safety latches were provided to hold the car should the cable come loose (a precaution taken by the other inclines) a small chip of metal was found in the throttle valve chest. The operating engineer, Charles Goble, stated that he could not stop the engines, claiming the throttle was frozen; the chip of metal was blamed. He admitted that some trouble with the machinery had been experienced earlier that morning but a few drops of oil had seemed to correct matters. Goble was held responsible since he was an experienced operator and should have reversed the engines and applied the winding drum brakes. The other employees on duty were charged with criminal neglect for failing to close the incline for a thorough inspection when the trouble was first noticed. It might be noted that while major catastrophes were perennially predicted and minor mishaps did occur, this was the single serious incline accident in the city's history.

loose. The car, now free from all restraints, lingered for an instant and then began its lightning like plunge to the bottom. The impact sounded like an exploding boiler; the air was filled with flying bits of glass, wood, and dust. The car body wrenched loose from the truck frame and hurled itself into a grocery store across the street. The roof of the car sailed down Main Street a full one hundred feet. Three passengers were killed outright; two more died within a few hours; and a sixth was dead several days later. The others escaped with injuries, as did two luckless pedestrians who were struck by

To restore public confidence it was decided to completely rebuild the incline. The old wooden trestle was demolished and the curious humpback grade was slightly reduced. New heavier engines were built by I. & E. Greenwald of Cincinnati. The track gauge was increased from 4 feet 10 inches to 6 feet 3 inches. The new plane was 860 feet long with a vertical lift of 275 feet. Open platforms

To restore public confidence after the 1889 accident, the incline was rebuilt with new machinery and other improvements. The scene is Mulberry Street near the upper end of Main Street.

measuring 36 feet by 8 feet returned the trucking of streetcars up and down the hill. Duplicate throttle and reversing mechanisms were installed as a safeguard against a repeat of the October disaster. The rebuilding of the plane was supervised by Milo D. Burke, an experienced civil engineer who earlier had directed construction of the Price Hill Incline.[24] The new plane was reportedly ready for testing in mid-December, but for reasons unknown to the writer it was not formally opened until February 9, 1890.

Three days after the incline's reopening William Howard Taft, then judge of the Superior Court of Cincinnati, decided a case which had been pending against the C.I.P. since the electric road went into service. The telephone company had complained that the single overhead wire with ground return used by the Mount Auburn line was interfering with phone service in the area. The telephone company also employed ground return and claimed priority rights, having installed its poles along Auburn Avenue in 1881 and 1882. The Kilgour family also controlled the phone company and was undoubtedly interested in prodding the case along to harass a new rival in the street railway business. Taft ruled in favor of the telephone company and ordered conversion to a double overhead trolley system within six months. This would constitute a major setback to the spread of electric railways in this country, for the single wire trolley was the cheapest electric distribution system yet devised. Fortunately for the industry, the Taft ruling was reversed by the Ohio Supreme Court on June 2, 1891, when it was demonstrated that properly bonded street railway tracks could carry the ground return without interfering with competing electrical systems.[25]

[24] *Cincinnati Gazette*, December 15, 1889; *Engineering News*, February 15, 1890.

[25] *The Electrical World*, Vol. 15, 1890, ran a series of articles on Judge Taft's decision.

Despite the twin setbacks of the incline wreck and the telephone lawsuit, Littell pressed on to extend the C.I.P. into the northern suburbs, convinced that expansion was the only hope of saving the C.I.P. as an independent operation. By March of 1889, the County Commissioners had agreed to the C.I.P.'s extension of tracks on Vine Street to Carthage. Work did not begin until the following spring, after the old part of Vine Street had been electrified. By May 1890 rails were distributed along the new line as far as St. Bernard, where a power plant was built at the B&O Railroad crossing of Vine Street. New stock worth $300,000 was issued, and there was talk of continuing the tracks on to Glendale. The, formal opening of the Carthage extension as far as St. Bernard was held on December 31, 1890, when at 8:00 p.m. a special train of cars carrying seven hundred guests traveled over the new line into the city. A brass band on the first car added a festive note to the event. The round trip took ninety minutes. A banquet was held in St. Bernard with toasts of success and thanks for the new enterprise. The mayor presented Littell with a handsome floral piece in the shape of a trolley car.[26] In time the extension was built out to Lockland.

A few months after the opening of the Carthage extension, H. H. Littell left Cincinnati to take on the management of the Buffalo trolley system. He maintained control as president of the C.I.P., but after his brother H. M. Littell departed the city in 1893 he called upon H. P. Bradford to manage the company. Bradford, formerly superintendent of the Little Rock, Arkansas lines, remained in charge until the property was sold five years later.

The new manager was faced with a series of difficulties soon after taking office, the most serious being the legal proceedings begun by the city in 1894.[27] The city claimed that the C.I.P. had no right to operate in the corporate limits under its steam railroad charter and was liable under the various street railway ordinances and car license taxes. Since it was not legally franchised, it was ordered to stop operation immediately. Again the company was saddled with a long, expensive lawsuit. While the suit was working its way through the courts from one appeal to the next, the C.I.P. fell onto the hard times that followed the Panic of 1893. By July 1895 interest payments on its mortgage bonds had to be suspended. A receiver was appointed in October. The city, eagerly pressing its case, started a second suit demanding that the C.I.P. remove its tracks from Liberty Street. Meanwhile, the first case had reached the Ohio Supreme Court, which ruled in favor of the city in December of 1896. The C.I.P. was able to obtain a temporary stay of dispossession from Judge Rufus B. Smith of Cincinnati. The company was given six months to right its affairs. Its fiscal matters were resolved a few weeks later and the receiver was dismissed. Littell talked again of rebuilding the company; more modern, electric cars would replace the pioneer Sprague equipment and new extensions would be built. The limit of Judge Smith's temporary order came and went. The C.I.P. continued to operate but the end was approaching and a public sale was in the air.

The Cincinnati Street Railway quietly offered to buy the line in early July 1897. Two plans were offered, one a complex cash and stock transfer, the other a straight cash offer of $350,000; both offers were rejected. The Cincinnati Street Railway was eager to absorb the C.I.P., now the sole

---

[26] Street Railway Review, February 1891, p. 38.

[27] Details of the city suit against the C.I.P are to be found in Arthur Espy, *Code of Franchises* (Cincinnati, 1914) ; Poor's *Manual of Railroads*, 1897, 1898; and various Cincinnati newspapers for the inclusive dates.

independent street railway operation in the city.[28] Another opportunity presented itself when the Fidelity Trust Company of Louisville offered to sell its considerable holding of C.I.P. bonds in the fall of 1897. The bank, anxious to unload the troublesome company, sensed that the natural monopoly inherent in public transit had already been consummated by the Kilgours. The bank asked for a decree of sale, which was granted by the U.S. Supreme Court in late February 1898. The sale was held on April 14.

Charles H. Kilgour bought the property for $278,000, considerably less than the Cincinnati Street Railway's offer of the previous year. That portion of the road from the Zoo to Lockland was turned over to the Mill Creek Valley Street Railway for operation; the city end went to the Cincinnati Street Railway Company. Kilgour was a director with a sizable interest in both corporations, which constituted in reality one company. On June 4 the incline was reported temporarily closed for repairs, but it never reopened. The Mount Auburn and city tracks of the C.I.P. were absorbed into the other routes of the Street Railway.

The northern portion of the line, however, was not so quietly absorbed. The citizens of Lockland were outraged at the take-over. Splitting the system in two parts, they declared, was a ruse by the Street Railway to collect a double fare.[29] The Street Railway was said to be behind the litigation that drove the C.I.P. out of business. In addition to this monstrous conspiracy, the new owners, by calling for a transfer and extra fare at the Zoo, were clearly violating the charters granted by several Mill Creek villages. The people of Lockland, who were skeptical of legal proceedings, decided to handle the matter in their own way. Late one

Sunday night in early June a gang of men stole out with picks and crowbars to tear up the tracks. They first visited the mayor of Lockland to ask for his sanction. This he would not do, but he advised them to "make a good job of it" if they meant to break the law. Besides pulling up the tracks at the far end of the line, a great barricade of rails and ties was piled up at Mill Creek Bridge. When the repair crew came out they were met by an angry mob armed with rocks and clubs. The local fire department threatened to hose down anyone who attempted to put the rails back. An injunction was served the next day, which further infuriated the crowd; those rails not previously disturbed were now torn loose. The battle continued throughout the summer. Carthage repealed the charter granted for the line's construction and ordered the removal of the tracks.

The argument was finally resolved in court. Service was restored and memories of the old Main Street line gradually faded. The line was made part of the regular Street railway system, with the transfer at the Zoo eliminated. In more recent times it became the Lockland route 78 and was one of the last Cincinnati streetcar lines to be abandoned. It retained one distinctive feature to the last year of service. All of the city's other trolley lines had the double trolley wire system—very rare in the United States— but the Lockland line from Mitchell Avenue north retained the single wire system which had been so valiantly fought for by the Cincinnati Inclined Plane Railway so many years ago.

[28] The two other sizable independand companies, the Mount Auburn Cable Railroad and the Mount Adams and Eden Park Inclined Plane Railway, were absorbed in 1896.

[29] *Cincinnati Commercial Tribune*, June 6, 7, 1898.

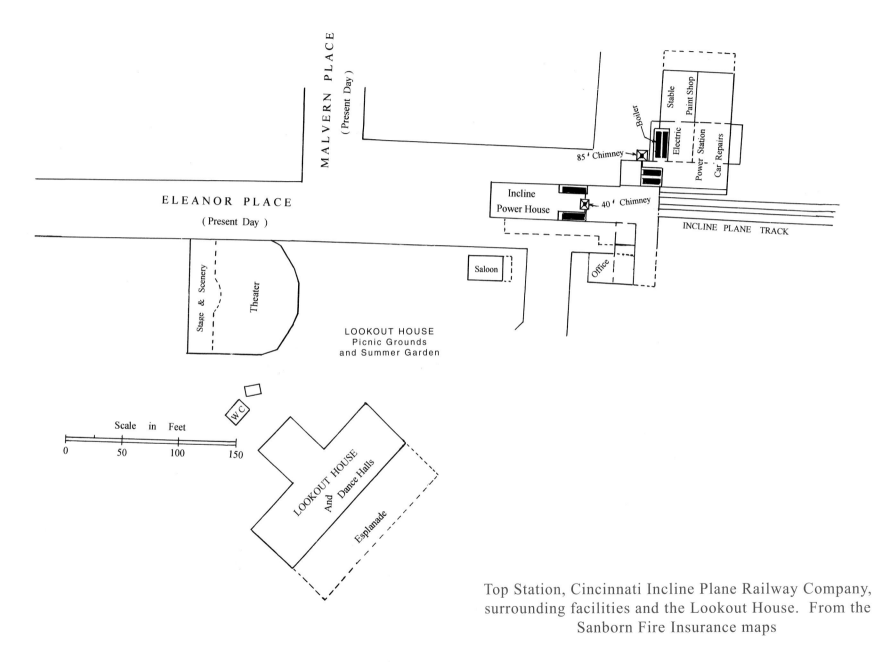

MALVERN PLACE
(Present Day)

ELEANOR PLACE
(Present Day)

Stage & Scenery

Theater

Saloon

Office

Incline Power House

85' Chimney

40' Chimney

Boiler

Electric

Stable

Paint Shop

Power Station

Car Repairs

INCLINE PLANE TRACK

LOOKOUT HOUSE
Picnic Grounds
and Summer Garden

Scale in Feet

0   50   100   150

W C

LOOKOUT HOUSE
And Dance Halls

Esplanade

Top Station, Cincinnati Incline Plane Railway Company,
surrounding facilities and the Lookout House. From the
Sanborn Fire Insurance maps

The Mt. Auburn Electric Railway as seen by a British Visitor

The Sprague Electric Company electrified the C.I.P. horsecar line from Fountain Square to the Zoo in 1889. The line used a single trolly wire with a ground return through the rails. Twenty cars offered service that ran in two-car trains. Each car had 2ea eight horsepower, 500vdc motors. The pinion gear was made of a red vulcanized fiber that wore as well as steel but was nearly noiseless. During non-rush hours, patronage was small and the cars averaged only about six to seven passengers per trip. Fifteen mph was the top speed possible on crowded city streets, however, efficient hand brakes could stop the cars in a short distance.

The generating plant was located next to the incline's top station, which was at the end of present-day Eleanor Place near Christ Hosiptal. Two 90 hp boilers supplied 90 psi of steam to the two electric generating engines. The boilers also supplied steam to the incline's winding engines. The power plant was near the middle of the line and power was transmitted along the route by heavy-duty transmission lines carried on iron and wooden poles. A Greenwald (Cincinnati) 150 hp engine with 18" x 42" cylinders was the main source of power. A smaller Ball engine (Erie, PA) was used as a back-up. Each drove a 50,000 watt Edison dynamo. The slower speed Greenwald engine drove a countershaft through a belt drive to achieve sufficient rpm's for the dynamo.

According to test runs in December 1889, the Greenwald consumed 2283 pounds of coal during an 8-1/2 hour period. A similar test with the Ball engine resulted in a fuel consumption of 3835 pounds. Assuming that an impartial test was conducted, the Greenwald engine was clearly the winner in terms of fuel economy.

A British visitor who rode the line twice a day, noted that the cars started and stopped abruptly. He seemed more amused than troubled by the perky little cars gyrations but said it caused frequent collisions with other men who stood on the rear platform to enjoy a cigar. He praised an advantage of electric traction that was often overlooked by transit riders; the electric lighting was not only brighter but gave off none of the heat or smell of the old-fashoned oil lamps. The Mt. Auburn system worked with perfection. Electric street car lines were becoming common and every large American city had at least one.

Adapted from *Engineering*, August 8, 1890, pg 151-152.

C.I.P. electric car at Mason and Eleanor Streets, enroute to the top station of the incline.

Chapter 3

The Mt. Adams & Eden Park Inclined Railway
"The Kerper Road"

The unexpected failure of Jay Cook & Company in September of 1873 swept America into the deep gloom of a severe depression. The Cincinnati money market was shaken; the Chamber of Commerce, trying to allay fears, solidly maintained, "to those of undoubted credit and the ordinary routine of safe business, there was ample means, while the speculator found money watching his movements with more than ordinary vigilance."[1]

Just a few months before the panic, E. M. Shield and his associates had incorporated on June 26, 1873, the Mt. Adams & Eden Park Inclined Railway. They proposed to build an incline, hardly longer than its pretentious title, up the hillside to Mt. Adams.

Mt. Adams had sprung up from a row of shacks dragged there after the Civil War and had grown into some semblance of a residential community. The smoke and heavy atmosphere of industrial Cincinnati had driven Professor Ormsby Mitchel's observatory to Mt. Lookout. Since the early 1870's, the residents had been petitioning for a decent carriage road to the hill. Times were ripe for development.

The Main Street Incline, opened the year before, had proved itself thoroughly practical, as had the Pittsburgh Incline, which began operations in 1870. Furthermore, there could be no doubt of the enterprise's success for Mr. Shield,

as he was a respected steam engineer and "a thoroughly practical man."[2]

The promoters of the incline seemed to have certain altruistic motives. Eden Park had been opened July 1, 1870, and only now was being developed into a public park. Mr. Longworth's vineyards were being replanted with trees, shrubs, and grass. A herd of deer was to be maintained. It would be a paradise indeed!

However, it was accessible only to the carriage trade, as few of the working class felt like scaling Mt. Adams after a fourteen-hour day. With an incline operating, all of the city's yeomanry might enjoy the benefits of the park.

Mr. Shield further stated that most of the right of way from Ida Street down the hillside to Lock Street had been acquired. He hoped to have the plane in operation by the next Industrial Exposition, scheduled for the fall of 1874.

Matters did not go as quickly or as easily as Shield had hoped. Money became tighter as the depression deepened, and difficulty was encountered in securing the rest of the right of way. He grew discouraged and dropped out of the project March 9, 1876 due to illness.

James E. Mooney, capitalist, puritan, tanner, was one of the original investors. He began to pour more of his capital into the enterprise and replaced Shield as its active head. He soon realized his other business affairs did not allow him sufficient time to devote to the flagging company.

He needed a capable lieutenant who had the necessary

---

[1] Report of the Cincinnati Chamber of Commerce 1874.
The original manuscript of this article is in the Mss. Collection of the *Cincinnati Historical Society* library in the Museum Center and is extensively documented with bibliographical footnotes.

[2] Ibid.

George B. Kerper

energy to bring the incline into existence. Mr. Mooney had made the acquaintance of a young Pennsylvanian named George B. Kerper, who had been sent on a goodwill tour of Europe by an association of American tanners. Recently back from St. Petersburg, Kerper accepted the invitation of Mooney and became the president of the Mt. Adams & Eden Park Inclined Railway.

Kerper was a small man in stature; energetic, adaptable, inclined to be plump, and bedecked with a great walrus mustache. In fact, he strongly resembled Louis Napoleon III.

In July of 1875, Kerper and his wife moved into a small house, which was located on Celestial Street not far from the site of the incline.

Construction had begun a few months after the charter was granted, but had languished. By May 11, 1874 the smoke-stack, brick work of the top depot and the boilers were completed.[3] Even the incline cars were finished. However, the machinery and trestle had yet to be built. Kerper pushed the project forward and began to formulate plans for a connecting system of street railway lines.

The incline was modeled on the pattern of the pioneer Main Street plane. Two parallel tracks, supported on a wooden trestle, ran down the hillside. Two cars, one for each track, were connected by a common cable, which was looped around two huge sheaves anchored securely in the incline house at the top of the hill. One car was at the top station when the other was at the bottom; or more simply, the weight of one car was balanced against the other. A set of winding drums powered by two stationary steam engines was in the engine room under the main floor of the incline house. Each car was attached to one of these drums by a hoisting cable. In effect, the machinery consisted of a heavy steam winch with a simple balance cable safety rig. Both winding drums and the safety sheaves were fitted with brakes; those of the latter were used only in times of emergency.[4]

In early March of 1876, preliminary tests were made and the machinery worked smoothly. On March 8th the first official run was made. Stockholders and other invited guests could ride up the plane on the "Nicholas Longworth" or the "Martin Baum" as the cars were named. The cars were specially built for incline service and were not merely horsecar bodies as on the Main, Elm, or the Price Hill planes.

[3] *Cincinnati Gazette*, May 11, 1874.
[4] For more technical data, see the Mt. Adams Incline 1875-1948 A Mechanical Report, by the author, in the Mss. Collection at the *Cincinnati Historical Society.*

The local papers considered it the most finished and best engineered of the four inclines then in operation. The depots were of brick and "finished in a modern style." Four days later, the plane was opened for regular service. A formal opening was planned for May when the Highland House, then under construction, was to be opened.

The company contemplated opening a steam narrow gauge railroad to the northwest and also planned to build a horsecar line through the park.

Before we become too immersed in the details of the Kerper Road, it might be well to briefly survey the street railway scene in the 1870's. There were several factors characteristic not only of the Cincinnati lines, but also of the industry as a whole. The street railway was a product of 19th century urbanization. It was autonomous, under capitalized, highly speculative, politically involved, and generally a poor investment. A city's street railways would be a hodgepodge of lines, built without a system, and as with Topsy, "just growed."

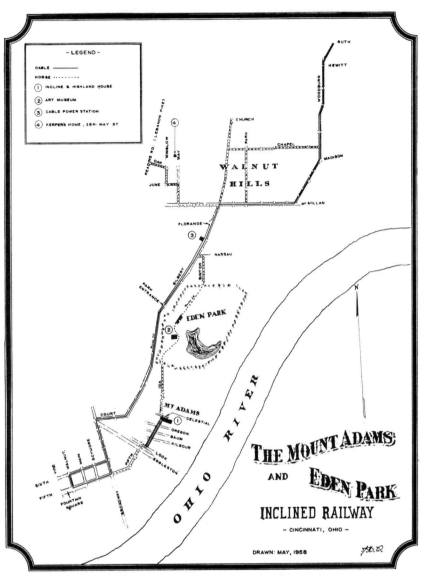

Map of the Kerper Road at its height in 1890.

The horse railway was entirely too expensive to operate. The size of the car was limited to the strength of the team and rarely surpassed a twenty-passenger capacity. A good horse cost $150.00 and was serviceable for not more than four years, in fact this would be the company's greatest investment. A mechanical means of power was desired.

In Cincinnati, to obtain a franchise, all an individual need do was to make a bid for the lowest rate of fare, agree to a gauge of five foot two inches, animal power, and build the lines along the route "suggested" by the city engineer. Thus, with about $200,000 and no particular knowledge, anyone might become a traction magnate. Public transportation was operated as a competitive proprietorship rather than a public utility.

Since franchise rights were loose and profits weak, there was little incentive for large capital investment nor any long range planning. However, if the lines could be consolidated into a strong system free of competition, it might prove a rich plum. This factor, coupled with rapid expansion and mechanical development, makes up the nucleus of our tale.

Cincinnati was a study in microcosm of the national scene. Lines were being built into the newly opened suburbs as the basin filled and became more industrialized. Not only the conventional street railway, but five incline planes were built, and a system of light steam narrow gauge railroads were racing out into the suburbs in the '70's.

Consolidation was in play also. In July of 1873 the better portion of the basin horsecar lines merged to form the Cincinnati Consolidated Street Railroad Company. Fittingly, the company's medallion-like seal on the stock certificate depicted Franklin and another founding father clasping hands; it was entitled "United We Stand, Divided We Fall!"

Style of track used by Mt. Adams & E.P horsecar lines.

According to the original grants, stairways were to be built leading from the streets cross to the plane, thus, hillside passengers might board the incline at various points. This would be a clumsy and dangerous operation. The city pressed the point, however, and entered suit in July 1876. The company agreed "provided they shall not be held liable for accidents…to individuals getting on or off the cars at these points." This only seems reasonable!

While the incline was running without fault, it was all but isolated. It ran from Lock Street, which was three blocks from the nearest car line, to the top of Mt. Adams. When the incline had opened, there were promises that a car would soon be running from the base of the incline to Fountain Square.

Kerper had hopes of avoiding the cost of building a new line by securing trackage rights over the Third Street Line into the city. Council and "the Consolidated" had different ideas; trackage rights were refused.

Permission was finally given by the Board of Public Works in September of 1876. Route 15 was established and the new line was to be built down Fifth Street into Fountain Square. Highland House was not completed by May nor was the grand opening celebration for the incline held. It was not until December 21, 1876 that the great Hilltop house was opened. Certainly, winter was a poor season for the opening; nevertheless, it created some enthusiasm. The *Enquirer* described it: "Its architectural design ... with which it is finished throughout will secure it general admiration."

Despite a fairly heavy snowfall, a sizable crowd appeared and were serenaded by Currier's Celebrated Reed Band. Numbers by Meyerbeer, Strauss, and Suppe were played, but the finale was written especially for the occasion by a Mr. S. Hook. It was entitled "Down the Incline."

Kerper had no intention of managing the Highland, for it was built for an investment and as an incentive to ride the incline. B. F. Starr leased the property.

Route 15 was progressing well, and cars were running by the spring of 1877. Plans to build a narrow gauge or a steam dummy line to Oakley were dropped in favor of a conventional horsecar line to be built through Eden Park.

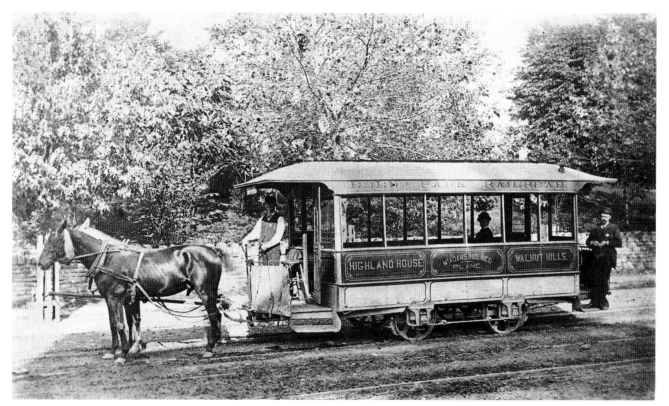

A Route 16 horse car at Oak and Lebanon Pike (Reading Road) in 1880.

carry one of the park drives (see p 52). However, lack of funds prevented the completion of the drive. This handsome design of James W. McLaughlin was a bit of a white elephant.[6] The franchise instructed: The "company . . . shall repair the stone bridge over the park entrance and erect thereon a safe and ornamental iron superstructure." Thus, through this odd mutation of cast iron and stone the level of the bridge was raised to the proper height for the line to cross the entrance of the park.

A 16-1/2 foot right of way was granted for which a rent of about $285.00 was charged. A $50.00 annual license fee per car was charged, and eight stations were to be erected on the park grounds.

In early April of that year ground was broken on Ida Street. An iron plate-way was built through the park. This was conventional horsecar trackage. Instead of laying expensive T-rail, wooden stringers covered by rolled iron strips were used (see preceeding page). A horsecar rarely weighed over two tons nor traveled at a speed greater than six miles per hour, so this construction proved quite adequate.

Kerper appealed to the egalitarian spirit of the city in that the general public should have easy access to the park. He was granted a charter November 16, 1877 for Route 16 but with certain stipulations.[5]

The route was typically vague; it was to run from the Ida Street Depot of the incline through the park grounds over the entrance bridge and "eventually" to Gilbert Avenue. The massive stone arched bridge at the park entrance had been built by the Park Board some years earlier and was meant to

[5] Code of Franchises, Arthur Espy, 1914.

[6] McLaughlin was the well known architect who designed the Art Museum, old Post Office, the former Public Library, Bellevue House and others.

51

Eden Park entrance bridge looking west toward Gilbert Avenue in about 1905. The iron upper section was removed in about 1947. The stone portion was demolished soon afterwards. The ticket to the right shows a horsecar passing over the same bridge.

The line was opened August 18, 1878, and was well received. It was first rate and with such easy grades that "the horses were able to trot all the way."[7]

Several years later Mr. P. Mulford, a visiting New Yorker, had nothing but praise for the line. ". . .Cincinnati on the breezy hills overlooking the city has instituted a park. And they allowed a horse railroad to run through their parks. Of course, older and eastern cities would never allow a horse railroad through their parks. It would be a sacrilege." He complains that in the east only the "rich" enjoy the public parks. He claimed that the Eden Park line was "...western, practical, progressive and sanitarian. A great many poor people after their week's work in the musty, ... Dirt ridden city, their lungs filled...with the emanations from 1,000 factories and 10,000 people about them, have little strength left to walk when they do, once a week, get into the park."[8] Mr. Mulford goes on with an inexhaustible array of adjectives to praise the democratic and epicurean rights of the worker to revel about in the park's grass.

Economically the line was not of much value, for until Grand Street [9] was completed, Route 16 was marooned within the limits of the park. It was not until the cars reached Walnut Hills (Peebles Corner) that any steady revenue passengers could be attracted. Park travel was fine, but it was only seasonal traffic.

The original capitalization of $250,000 in 1873 had proved long since inadequate. The incline machinery and equipment had cost $90,000; the property $110,000. Route 15 was built for $17,000 and the original cost of Highland House was $50,000. Before the Eden Park Line could be built the capital value was doubled to $500,000 in 1877.

Possibly the reader is a bit wearied by the frenzy of building, franchises, and finances; a little relaxation at the Highland House is in order. The season has changed, it is spring in the late 1870's. A contemporary newspaper reports the impressions made upon a visitor to the city; "he catches a glimpse from his carriage windows as he is driven to his hotel of the dark amphitheater of hills surrounding the city proper on three sides, and in some turn of a street corner suddenly bursts upon his vision a spectacle that makes him start with an exclamation of surprise, wonder and delight. High up against the sky he sees a long, symmetrical line of lights glittering against the dark background of the skies; above that line another, above that another, and so on in narrowing ranks, until the pyramid is topped with a great white, dazzling blaze from an electric light that sends a broad belt of radiance across the city, and even turns the church spires into silver points away beyond the yellow Ohio upon the Kentucky shore. Perhaps through the pauses in the street uproar the sound of gay music floats down, brilliantly lighted cars go up and down between the dark city level and the fairy palace up there against the sky, and in the sheen of the thousands of twinkling lights, banners and streamers can be seen flapping in the breeze, when not a breath of air is stirring down in the city.

"'What is it?' asks the stranger in wonder. 'The Highland House,' is the answer."

The Highland House is ". . .where the cool breezes always blow in the hottest and most sultry summer days, where the best beer of the world flows perennially, where the delicious music sounds almost continually, and where the prettiest girls in America promenade of an evening."[10]

The 4th of July was the biggest day experienced by the hilltop houses. The Independence Day celebration of

[7] *Cincinnati Gazette*, August 19, 1878.
[8] *Cincinnati Gazette*. May 22, 1880.
[9] Now Sinton Avenue.

[10] *Cincinnati Commercial*, March 31, 1878.

Highland House as it appeared when new. *Scientific American Supplement*, April 20, 1878.

'*America*'; reportedly the largest in the country."

After sunset the fireworks display started with "George Washington on Horseback" and "The Eruption of Vesuvius." Few people could enjoy the spectacle for many of the patrons were standing on the tables blocking the view.

The Lookout House, not wishing to be outdone, advertised: "The third, last, and only genuine living white whale! See it today, for tomorrow it may be dead."

1877 was a near riot at the newly opened Highland. Seemingly everyone in the city insisted on celebrating the day there. The little cars of the incline could not begin to accommodate the crowd that was building up on Lock Street. The police arrived. The impatient crowd began swarming up the hillside on foot.

The two great towers and the many gable poles were beplumed with flags and streamers. An enormous white flag, emblazoned with "The Highland House," floated from the rear tower. Inside the waiters could not move. The thirsty crowd sat at their wet tables waiting to be served. Out on the "Belvedere" two brass bands blasted away at one another. Later in the evening Professor Harry Gilbert prepared to make a "grand balloon" ascension...in his mammoth airship

Fortunately, not all days were so trying; often as not a quiet refreshing atmosphere could be found. In the afternoon the place was all but deserted. One could enjoy a dark beer or a good Morlein Lager and a smoke, plus all the scenery and air to be had. Comfortably seated in a wicker chair the viewer might watch one of the White Collar Line steamers leisurely pull into the stream, all white, and lay back a great cloud of black coal smoke as she steamed up river. Everything would appear distant, innocent, and Arcadian.

The Highland was the scene of conventions and meetings. Roscoe Conkling delivered an address to an audience of 20,000 Republicans, whose only disappointment was the brevity of his speech. The National Grain Congress met there, as did a narrow gauge railroad convention.

In the late 70's and the early 80's the Highland was known as a place of social importance. The Theodore Thomas Concerts brought a hint of culture. [11]

We shall leave the Highland for the moment with the parting thought that if we were an adult Cincinnatian of the period it would be our duty to consume forty gallons of beer per annum!

Kerper's ambition was "a little machine that knew no rest." He obtained permission to push Route 16 beyond Eden Park on to Avondale. Work commenced in November of 1879. The line would run from Grand Street up Gilbert Avenue to McMillan east to May Street, and then down Oak to terminate at the Lebanon Pike (Reading Road). There seemed nothing unique in the move, merely the extension of another horsecar line.

There was more to the scheme than the extension. The incline was to be closed and radically remodeled. Machinery barely five years old was to be scrapped.

George B. was exasperated by the folly of operating two stub lines from the top and bottom depots of the incline. In eliminating the awkward transfer by rebuilding the plane, the team, horsecar, and all could be loaded on the open platform and lowered to the city below. The North Hudson County Railway (New Jersey) had pioneered such a funicular railway six years before with great success. Of course, the Price Hill people had opened their freight plane the year before, but it was used only by drays and not by public passenger carriers. This was an intelligent,

Henry Marcus Lane

if not an original application.

Work began November 2. Since the incline would be down the Highland House was closed, but at no particular loss for in the winter seasons the great house was all but a morgue.

The pretentious baroque dome and the jetty-like boarding docks came down; in fact, the whole front section of the top depot disappeared. It was replaced by the high pitched gables of the Gothic Revival facade which was to be familiar to all Cincinnatians for the next six generations. The handsome little incline cars, "The Nicholas Longworth" and "The Martin Baum," joined the original winding machinery as scrap.

Henry Marcus Lane, son of Philander P. Lane and a recent graduate of M.I.T., designed and supervised the erection of the new machinery. It was built in his father's shop, the legendary Lane & Bodley Company, then the largest machine shop west of the Alleghenies. Lane, a gifted, autocratic little man, was to figure largely in the affairs of Kerper and his domain in the next few years.

It had been hoped that the work could be finished in four to six weeks. However, it was not until late April of 1880 that the open platforms began rumbling over the Mt. Adams hillside. The *Commercial's* reporter seemed more heartened by the Highland's reopening than by the triumphs of cable, steam, and steel. He said, "it is good for one to sip beer at the Highland, not especially for the beer, but because it is a part of the landscape...a thing in keeping with the scene." From the Highland you look down upon the busy

[11] A Pavillion House was built to the east of the Belvedere in May of 1877 for the Thomas Concerts.

city and catch a perspective of life. It is good to get away far enough to do this sometimes. And you leave a little regretfully coming down to take up the plain prose of life again, while Aris regales you with reminiscences of the lovely summer nights of last year when all Cincinnati sat on the terrace and sipped iced beer, and listened entranced to the Thomas orchestra - to the dreamy, delicious music of Strauss and the haunting symphonies of Beethoven. The picture lingers - those summer evenings that were each a veritable mid-summer night's dream." [12]

One factor usually neglected when speaking of the open platforms is the added revenues they brought. Not only the company's horsecars were "trucked," [13] but also any drayman who might present himself with his cart and be willing to pay the tariff. I have no knowledge of revenue cards of the Mt. Adams Company, but the Price Hill plane at that time charged 80 cents and up, depending on the size of the team and wagons. This traffic was lucrative. Charles Schnittgner, former employee of the old Bellevue plane (Elm Street) recalls teams lined up for several blocks waiting for the incline to open up at five in the morning.

Possibly the reader wonders if the story of the Kerper road is any more than the tale of a marginal horsecar line operation or the weak romance of the Highland House. This, quite probably, is all that it would have been without the extraordinary character of its President. The Mt. Adams & Eden Park Railway became the city's second largest street railway, and did, though admittedly never too seriously, rival the "Consolidated." The other independents were either swallowed up or meekly kept within their limited one-line operations. But not the Mt. Adams Company. It ventured forth and if it did not always fulfill its grandiose dreams, it

[12] Cincinnati Commercial, April 26, 1880.
[13] This is an incline term for lifting or hoisting a vehicle up or down the plane.

did give Johnny Kilgour and the "Consolidated" many an uneasy moment.

Seemingly there are no real factors to differentiate the other independents from the Mt. Adams Company, save one — its bold, energetic president, George B. Kerper.

Granted, this is, at best, a hypothesis, and may be even less, for practically nothing survives Kerper but contemporary newspaper accounts. However, if you will concede these accounts as reflections of public opinion, we are on the way toward proof. Mind, not absolute truth, but rather public opinion, for what is held to be true in history and what may actually be true are often two distinct matters. Of course, one could be safe and write nothing but a dull chronicle of the events beginning May 21, 1878.

Kerper's genius lay not in a towering intellect, but rather in his capacity to capture the public imagination. He could be a bit of a huckster, a demagogue, but he never burlesqued to the point of the ridiculous. He did accomplish this: the working public championed him as a friend and a benefactor. He granted them voluntary fare reductions, heated winter cars, and more rapid transit. Whether this was motivated by purely competitive factors, or not, the public believed him a magnanimous patron.

They found in him also a lovable character, and were fond of bestowing nicknames on him. The men of the company called him "The Little Giant;" he was known as "King Kerper," and with the coming of the cable car as "Kable Kar Kerper." His legend had built to such a point that when he retired a grateful public gave him a sterling silver service.

The company had experienced no particular rivalries in these early formative years. True enough, Mayor Robert A. Johnston of Avondale had proposed and actually chartered a company to build an incline plane around the hillside from the Mt. Adams plane. [14] This plane was never built.

There was one other potential source of competition, the Walnut Hills & Cincinnati Street Railroad had been chartered as Route No. 10 in 1872. It was to be built up Gilbert Avenue, whose broad section was just being paved at that time. The line had not amounted to much. The steep grade required a practice known as "doubling." An extra team of horses was hitched to the car at the bottom of the hill and then helped tow it up the grade. The team was led by a boy who would in turn ride back down the grade to help the next car up. The trips up Gilbert Avenue hill alone consumed one half-hour. The cost of doubling all but broke the company. A Mr. Paxton hoping to build a competing line spoke of Route 10: the "...Walnut Hills Railroad has already fallen to pieces with age. When this ordinance (his new line) was projected, they bought a little lumber. When it passed the first board they got a car or two, and now they are so much agitated that it is probable they will buy a horse."

The line took on a grim prospect in the spring of 1880. A new combine was in the works. Kerper attempted to purchase Route 10 in May, but without success.

June 22, the Cincinnati Consolidated Street Railroad, the Storr and Sedamsville Street Railway, the Cincinnati and Spring Grove Avenue line, and the Cincinnati and Clifton Incline Plane Company (Elm Street) merged to form the Cincinnati Street Railway Company. The Walnut Hills and Cincinnati Railway was brought into the syndicate at eight cents on the dollar.

The Little Giant was not too concerned about this for his Routes 15 and 16, plus the incline, offered much more pleasant and speedy service to Walnut Hills via Eden Park than the dusty journey up Gilbert Avenue.

Pressures were brought to bear; in October the "Consolidated" [15] bought out the Lebanon and Xenia Turnpike (Reading Road) as far as Avondale. They began work on a carline; there were now "Consolidated" car lines running parallel to the Mt. Adams route. The *Commercial* reported, "It is generally supposed that the object of the railway company in purchasing the pike is for the purpose of coercing Mr. Kerper's road into the consolidation. [16] Colonel Bullock, former superintendent of the old "Consolidated," quietly visited Mr. James A. Mooney and tried to persuade him to sell out from under Kerper. Mooney indignantly refused.

The next move of Kilgour was ingenious. He proposed to build a cable railway up Gilbert Avenue. This was a daring move, for it was generally believed that while the cable might be a success in the mild climate of San Francisco, it would prove a total failure in any city experiencing a severe winter. It wasn't until the year 1882 when the Chicago Cable opened that these fears were disproved. [17] He backed up his proposal by inviting Mr. Henry Casebolt, a cable railway expert of San Francisco, to build an experimental line in the city. Casebolt is probably better remembered for his invention of the overhead cable street railway than his ingenious "balloon car."

Kerper quickly recognized the significance of the project. If Casebolt could successfully build his cable road it would cut the hill time of Route 10 in half. This would ruin the traffic on Route 16.

[14] *Cincinnati Commercial*, March 13 and 16, 1875. Franchise of the Cincinnati, Walnut Hills, Avondale, and Pleasant Ridge Street and Incline Plane Railway was granted December 28, 1874. *The Code of Franchises*, Arthur Espy, 1914

[15] Kerper and the newspapers insisted on calling the Cincinnati Street Railway by its old corporate title, the Cincinnati Consolidated Railway. This practice persisted well into the 1890's.

[16] *Cincinnati Commercial*, October 3, 1880.

[17] *Cable Railways of Chicago*, by G.W. Hinton 1954. The general belief was that the cable slot and conduit would fill with ice preventing the movement of the cable or grip.

The matter was drawn out for some time in the meetings of the Board of Public Works and its committee on street railways. Kerper protested that if the cable cars ran north of Grand Street on Gilbert Avenue, they would push his slower horsecars off the track. (Both Route 10 and 16 used the same tracks on this section.) Mooney stated that the slotways would be "embarrassing" for carriage traffic. And so the arguments went. Superficial, yes, but if the rival line were built, this might well prove to be the death throes of the Mt. Adams Company. Kerper was stalling for time, time to plan his counterattack.

In this instance, Kerper was no better than any manager of the period. He was obstructing for purely competitive reasons, and was justly denounced at the time for it. However, the ensuing campaign was a brilliant illustration of Kerper's ability to capture public support.

In September of 1881 Kerper made a proposition more startling than that of introducing the cable car. He proposed to build a giant cable belt line across McMillan Street, down Vine Street hill, on to Third Street, at the site of the proposed new Union Depot, and then up the incline to Walnut Hills. Kerper planned to string a neat loop of Mr. Roebling's wire rope around the neck of the "Consolidated." He would hang them with their very own device!

He spoke to the Board of Public Works concerning the cable for Route 10 with a hint of irony, "I was told that we were standing in the way of a great public improvement, and must yield. We resolved to take your advice and become the public benefactors, by offering to build an extension and adopt the cable system."[18]

Late in October, handbills were passed in Corryville and Walnut Hills. They were innocently entitled, "Eden Park Railroad, Route 16," however, they were explosive in content. "We invite the public and especially the citizens of Mt. Auburn and Walnut Hills to aid us in cinching the good work in progress by giving us their united support in carving out the grandest enterprise ever offered the people, namely our extension via McMillan Street and Vine Street hill.

"The object of the Consolidated Company is obvious to all, they desire to wipe out competition by the consolidation of competing lines and to throttle our extension by offering a temporary reduction in fares." The "Consolidated" was further characterized as a "grasping monopoly." A meeting of protest should be held; the bill was signed by George B. Kerper.

A meeting was held October 29th in Mt. Auburn at Buehler's Hall. The Kerper plan was heartily endorsed. The Little Giant gave the crowd a passionate address, in which he warned the citizens of the all-consuming ogre. "It now rests with the public and the city authorities to say whether, with the power they have controlling nearly all the territory in the city and suburbs, they shall succeed in crushing out the little competition that still exists. We believe the people fully understand their

This card offered free transportation to the owner and his Lady

[18] *Cincinnati Commercial*, September 30, 1881.

motives and we entered this fight as we have in all our enterprises in the past —confident of success."[19] In effect Kerper was personifying the Consolidated as a corporate devil; which made it easy for the simplest of minds to join him in his crusade against the monster.

This man Kerper was becoming a danger, he could not be bought out, frightened by the specter of the cable, and now he was giving the Consolidated painful publicity. Superintendent C. G. Gove resorted to the old trick of the rate war. He would bankrupt the Kerper road. Fares on Route 10 and the new Avondale line were cut to three cents.

Kerper used this against them stating that it was merely a device to throttle his company. "I see Mr. Gove says, in an interview in the Gazette, that the three cent fare was done in the interest of the public. I am glad to know that the Consolidated Company have changed their tactics, and I hope that they will show their earnestness in this by giving to the entire people of the city the same kind of interest (low fares)." He added, bitterly: "The people of Mt. Adams and Corryville have been working for a year to get a six and one fourth cent fare, but their interests in the public don't lie in that direction." The Consolidated was roundly indicted; "Yes, Sir, if the people expect a permanent reduction in fares they will have to stick to us. You know, they know (wave of hand), everybody knows how they gobbled up the 8th Street, the Vine Street, the Sedamsville and the Clifton lines, and the Elm Street Incline, and are the people along these routes any better off for it? Not one cent, Sir, not one cent. We lessened the time to Walnut Hills and compelled them to similar steps. They were selling only thirteen tickets for a dollar on the Gilbert Avenue line, and we made them give sixteen for the same sum. We introduced stoves for winter comfort and made them do it also."[20]

Barely a week after Kerper's public meeting, the Cincinnati Street Railway called for the citizens to mass at the Corryville Fire House. Mr. Kilgour would show that he, too, was a public benefactor. He proposed to open the Vine Street hill line and grant reduced fares to that area of the city.

The Board of Public Works was being petitioned by the Citizens committee that resulted from the Kerper meeting. All to the discomfort of the Consolidated. Kilgour could not see why his generous proposal should not be cordially received.

After a perfunctory reading of the Consolidated's proposal, John Kilgour rose to address the meeting. However, he was met by catcalls and a general demand for Kerper to speak instead. Kilgour blustered that this meeting had been called by the Street Railway and then stated his case. "At the close of his remarks there were (again) loud calls for Mr. Kerper." From the back of the hall the Little Giant reluctantly strolled to the speaker's platform. He modestly stated that he came to the meeting merely as an observer; after all, had not Mr. Kilgour invited all interested citizens? He then launched into a spirited attack of the Consolidated. He was frequently interrupted by "loud cheers from the crowd."[21]

A few minutes later, the citizens committee returned to the platform and, much to the pleasure of the assemblage, reported in favor of the Kerper plan! Nor was this all, Colonel Jones, one of Kilgour's lieutenants, was severely criticized for his acts of bad faith. When the good Colonel rose to defend himself, he was greeted by cheers which the *Enquirer* reporter deemed it best not to print. It need hardly be added that the Street Railway suffered an ignominious

[19] *Cincinnati Commercial,* October 28, 1881.

[20] *Cincinnati Commercial,* October 28, 1881.

[21] *Cincinnati Enquirer,* November 9, 1881.

defeat. Hereafter, Kilgour left the courting of public favor to the Little Giant.

The issue was not yet resolved; all the public favor in the city could not completely alter the hard economics of the struggle. The rate war continued, and was more to the distress of the Mt. Adams Company. The Street Railway could cushion their losses on the Gilbert Avenue and Reading Road lines by the profitable operation of the rest of their system. This could go on indefinitely until the Mt. Adams Company was bankrupt. Kerper admitted his stockholders were dissatisfied. The enterprise had just shown its first profits, a bare six per cent the year before. For better than five years his investors had waited for some return and now the rate war seemed sure to kill that too.[22]

The Consolidated did not enjoy its losses, even though it could afford them, and most certainly was vexed by its loss of public prestige.

Rumors of a compromise were in the air in early December. Some said the officials of both companies had held a secret meeting at the Highland. The market was excited, large amounts of unsubscribed Mt. Adams stock were put on sale and were eagerly bought up.

The exact nature of the agreement was made public December 4, 1881. The terms were simple: the Mt. Adams Company would buy Route 10 from the Street Railway for $270,000; $230,000 was to be in Mt. Adams common stock and the balance in cash. Two members of the seven-man board of directors were to be from the Cincinnati Street Railway Company. So it was resolved, Kerper had the Gilbert Avenue line; Kilgour owned a share of the Mt. Adams Company and had two of his men on the board.

---

[22] Kerper later admitted they weren't making operating expenses on the four-cent fare. Six to eight per cent was about par for horsecar lines, which were generally poor earners.

Ultimately, the compromise led to the absorption of the Kerper Road by the Kilgour interests. Immediately, it postponed an outright consolidation move, which the Street Railway had hoped for. Kerper felt that there was little danger for he, Mooney, Lemont and their associates held over fifty per cent of the company's paper. They felt they could count on another twenty-five per cent of the stockholders to be absolutely loyal to them. However, Kilgour and the other members of his board steadily bought Mt. Adams certificates during the next few years. The plot was set, the drama could follow but one avenue; and that led to absorption.

The compromise meant to the public what you might expect, an immediate restoration to the ten cent fare on Routes 10 and 16! The McMillan-Vine Street Hill extension: Kerper continued to talk of this reassuringly, but no cable cars were seen by the Corryville folk for six years hence.

There followed a welcome lull. The horsecars continued their leisurely travels over the light iron of the Eden Park route. In the summer the tiny fourteen passenger cars brushed aside the bright green foliage. On the front platform stood the driver, costumed in dark trousers, a vest, and a white shirt, which, while buttoned, was without a tie. More than likely, he would be sporting a derby. In the winter, this same carefree fellow would have his legs wrapped in gunnysacks and would swing his arms, reins in hand, to and fro to keep up his circulation. The great black machinery at the Incline wound and unwound its heavy cables stoically. Up and down the hillside, platforms would travel immune to the emotion, life, and misery they daily viewed.

The Little Giant was very busy; meetings, conventions, banquets, these were all his delights. In 1882 he went, with John Kilgour's blessing, as the Ohio Street Railway Association's representative to the organizational meeting of the American Street Railway Association. He was well received and voted a Vice-President. Several years later, in 1888, probably the high point in the little man's career, he was elected President of the association. The verbatim reports of this organization offer flowery bits of oratory and lengthy discussions on the problems and future of the industry. These ranged from effective methods to save employees from falling into the bad ways of the Knights of Labor to the introduction of electrical power.

In this interim, the scheme of converting Gilbert Avenue to a cable line lay dormant. The successful operation of the Chicago cable had established the plausibility of such a system in a cold weather climate. It illustrated another fact, the great cost of such a project. A single tracked cable line cost better than $100,000 per mile, and that was less power equipment and cars. This was far more than the Mt. Adams Company could afford. At the same time, the company could not very well afford not to convert. The costs of horse car operation were prohibitive, and the line was becoming clogged. Walnut Hills was the fastest growing suburb in the city at that time, and by 1883 nearly 10,000 passengers per day were traveling over Route 10. It took nearly thirty minutes for a horsecar to grind up the long Gilbert Avenue grade, which must have proved exasperating even to the most leisurely of Victorians. Kerper reported to his stockholders that the San Francisco cables showed operating expenses forty to fifty per cent below those of competing horsecar lines.[23]

Kerper also knew that when the traffic reached five thousand passengers per day it was economical to expend the capital for the cable system.

Henry Lane, the designer of the machinery for three of the city's inclines, reappeared. Lane, for all his eccentricities, such as his insistence on being called "Master" by his shopmen, was a gifted engineer: He claimed he could design and build a cable railway at a fraction of the cost of the Chicago line. Kerper consented to the building of an experimental line on May Street. In the summer of 1884 Lane constructed the road based on the Johnson "ladder cable and sprocket wheel system of cable railways."[24] Seemingly, it was not all that was expected, for Lane abandoned the project and designed a system based on a more conventional model.

In the November preceding the May Street experiment, Lane and S. M. Lemont, a friend of Kerper and a director of the Mt. Adams Company, drafted the preliminary papers to incorporate the "Traction Cable Company."[25] This was to be a construction company whose intent was to contract and build cable railways. H. M. Lane would be the chief engineer and would assign all his patents and designs to the company. A corporation was actually set up in August of 1885 called the Lane National Cable Railway Construction Company. George B. Kerper and John Kilgour were taken in as new partners. It was possibly by more than a coincidence that the Gilbert Avenue contract was awarded to this company. Several years later Kilgour also decided to have Lane build his Vine Street cable. All of this may smack of Credit Mobilier tactics, but it may be viewed in another manner. Both Kerper and Kilgour had large personal investments in their respective street railways, and were not very likely to cheat themselves. It was certainly to their advantage to see that the company built them a sound railway.

Before we proceed into the intimacies of the cable railway's anatomy, it might be well to discuss its principle. Very simply, the car is propelled by gripping a cable, which moves through a tunnel or conduit beneath the surface of

[23] Horse Car - 25 cents per mile, Cable Car - 12 cents per mile.

[24] The Street Railway Journal, May 1895.

[25] All discussion of the Lane National Cable Construction Company is based on the papers of that corporation, courtesy of Miss Caroline Hein of the Cincinnati Transit Company.

the street. The cable is endless in that it is a great loop. It is wrapped around large driving wheels, powered by stationary engines, which put it in motion. It is guided around the curves by a suitable arrangement of pulleys or sheaves. The grip is a simple jaw-like device, which when tightened grasps the cable, and thus propels the car. When the grip is open, the cable merely slides through it and the car remains stationary.

All of this sounds elementary, and in principle, it is. However, the design of such a system is another matter. The management of some forty tons of unruly wire rope traveling at eight miles per hour or better, is no small matter. Add to this the need for stability, drainage, and exact alignment, and there are some very real technical problems. The effect of the climate on the roadbed was particularly troublesome. Centered in the track was the slotway through which the shank of the grip passed to be attached to the car. Due to the summer's heat, the slots would expand, thus closing, and impeding the grips shank. In the winter, it would contract, thus opening a dangerous gap to catch narrow buggy wheels, etc. The cable was an expensive item, costing about $1,400 per mile. The more it was unduly flexed or bent, the more rapidly it wore out. The engineer had to caress and make easy its every movement to increase its life. The cable was treated with pitch and linseed oil to lubricate and keep it flexible.

These factors, beyond the obvious ability to produce an operable system, were met by Lane. Even more important, he could build a line for less than a third of regular costs. Still, the cost of converting the entire Gilbert Avenue line seemed too great, and also Lane's system had not yet been proven. Therefore, it was decided to convert only the hill portion of Gilbert Avenue from Court Street to Nassau Street. Either end of the line would operate as a conventional horsecar road. The horsecar would pull up to the bottom of

View of Lane's detachable grip from *Street Railway Gazette,* October 1886

the grade and while still in motion, a detachable grip would couple onto the bottom of the car, and propel it up the grade. Similar operation took place for cars descending the grade. The horses were detached momentarily before the grip grappled on. A "T" shaped slot ran the length of a coupling bracket secured on the underside of the car. A corresponding T was milled in the top of the grip mechanism. This rested on small rollers on top of the slotway. As the car rolled over the grip the T was grappled by the bracket and a heavy latch fell in place locking it tight. Then, while the car was still in motion, a connecting rod was coupled to the grip wheel, which was mounted on the front platform. The conversion from horse to cable car was accomplished in twenty to thirty seconds. The grip was released from the car at the top of the hill. A team was hitched on the fly, and the trip was thus continued without a stop. This certainly was unique operation in the annals of the industry, and was of great credit to Lane's engineering ability. Construction began in April of 1885. A trench 42 inches deep and nearly five feet wide was dug. Great cast iron yokes, 250 pounds each, were mounted on six-inch concrete footings and spaced five feet apart. The slotway was bolted to the top of these yokes. The rails were also anchored to the yokes by means of angle iron struts. This alone formed a rigid roadway. Yet about sixteen inches of concrete was poured around the base of the yokes. This not only secured the structure, but formed the bottom of the conduit. Here is where Lane practiced some economy measures. Instead of using concrete to form the walls of the conduit, he substituted heavy creosoted planks and rammed earth against them. Regular street paving covered over this fill between the rails and slotway. The method was not only economical, but proved most satisfactory. It was used on the other lines he was later to build in Denver, Providence, R. I., and other cities.

Other economies were achieved by clever designing. Much drilling and fitting were eliminated by use of keys rather than bolts in securing the bottom of the slot rails to the yokes. The driving machinery was possibly some of the most simple ever designed. The main drive gear and sheaves were in one unit. The gearing was as simple as possible; a single pinion drove the main gear. The more typical driving machinery, say of Poole and Hunt of Baltimore, one of the bigger builders of such equipment, consisted of a separate gear-sheave system and also of tandem drive sheaves coupled by side rods. This was infinitely more complex and expensive.

The work progressed with amazing speed. By July the 4th, the date that Kerper had hoped to open the line, the giant 22-ton cable was laid. A *Commercial* reporter, writing in the third person, described the scene. "Eight great draught horses strode down the hill from the machinery plant, at the intersection of Grand Street and Gilbert Avenue, to the corner of Court Street, dragging the cable by one end and laying it in the west track tunnel. But it took sixteen big horses to continue the service, after the turn had been made at Court Street, pulling the cable up the long weary hill more than a mile, and laying it in the east track tunnel.

Along the line down the hill flagmen were stationed to signal back when the horses should start after any unnecessary halt. The great round mass of wire rope revolved swiftly and the cable laid out splendidly, as the march of men and horses down the hill commenced and continued. The cable hummed faintly between the yokes in the tunnel and one following was slightly reminded of San Francisco and Chicago.

"The last the writer saw of this interesting cable laying was the stately march up the hill of the sixteen great horses. He watched them until the big clouds of dust hid them. But he knew by the faint humming of the cable in the tunnel that they were marching on."

The opening was four days later. On July 17, 1885, the Little Giant celebrated the completion of the first cable railway in Ohio.[26] The members of the Board of Public Works toured the line and then adjourned to the Highland. During the luncheon several impromptu speeches were offered and were followed by the reports of smashed glasses.

Several months before the work commenced on the line, a gentleman by the name of A. H. Lighthall arrived in the city. He was a "large man, of full habit" and was not modest in proclaiming his knowledge of cable railways. He

[26] The Cincinnati Street Railway started constuction of a cable line on Spring Grove Avenue in the spring of 1885. It was, however, stopped by a court injunction.

set himself up in a sumptuous parlor suite at the Gibson House. Anyone that might cross his path was treated to a lecture on the virtues and intricacies of the cable railway. The listener was shown a graphic panorama of Mr. Lighthall's inventive genius via drawings, models, and a library of engineering treatises; all of which he carried about the country in several great trunks.

Despite his florid manner, Kerper and Kilgour were impressed and invited him to join them in the Lane National Cable Construction Company. They also enfranchised him to sell his and Lane's system to other cities.

Lane looked over Mr. Lighthall's patents and designs and found them worth while. Some of his work was incorporated in the Gilbert Avenue Line.

In mid-October of 1885, Mr. Lighthall suddenly disappeared. The manager of the Gibson House discovered that his check was no good. The next news of Mr. Lighthall was from a St. Louis friend of Charles Kilgour who had given the inventor a sum of money, and then seen him no more. He was finally traced to New York but the Gibson House received no satisfaction, for other creditors were ahead of them. Kerper and Kilgour remained silent on the subject. Several months later the Little Giant quietly bought up Lighthall's holdings in the Cable Construction Company at a sheriff's sale. The *Commercial* sensibly concluded that, while Mr. Lighthall may have been an adept engineer, this in no way sanctioned his deceptive treatment of Cincinnati's more credulous capitalists.

The road was entirely successful mechanically. The cable had lasted 15 months. Six months was considered very good service by most lines. Operationally the Lane system was sound. But the actual costs of operation for Route 10 had risen by $500.00 per month. This was easily explained. Two teams of horses had to be maintained for each car; one team at either end of the cable. Also, temporary stables were built at both ends of the cable section. As previously stated, the cable had been built as an experiment. Lane proved that he could build not only an operable line, but do so at a price that the Mt. Adams Company could afford, *i.e.* $30,000 per mile. Now the real economies of cable traction could be realized. Plans were made to extend the southern end down Broadway and into the city. The northern end would be extended out Woodburn Avenue. The completed road would be about four miles in length. A turntable would be installed at the far end of the line.

Work began, in the spring as usual, in April of 1886. Problems of every variety developed. The hill section had been just one mile and a half, but now the cable was more than doubled in length and there were to be two cables. The length of a cable is directly proportional to the contrariness of its behavior. Also, the more curves the shorter and more unruly is the cable's life. The Street Railway Gazette (October, 1886) stated that it was ... "a route with more curve and difficulties to overcome, in its operation, than any cable road in existence ... ." There had been contention with the city about the construction of the line on Gilbert Avenue. Its thoroughfare was wide, and the digging of the trenches and the resulting mounds of earth did little to interfere with the traffic. However, such construction on Broadway, Walnut, and Fifth and Sixth Streets was another matter. Many just complaints were voiced. Here again, Kerper's personality entered. The *Commercial* reported .... "George is so personally fascinating that the Board (of Public Works) regarded it as a doubtful expediency and effect to cite him before it, lest he should joke and cajole them out of their official indignation just then at the boiling point."[27]

[27] *Cincinnati Commercial*, October 10, 1886.

To say the least, Lane had confidence in his own ability. He also had the habit of overtaxing the abilities of his plant. The job of building such a quantity of machinery was more than the shops of Lane and Bodley Company could manage. Much of the work had to be sub-contracted. Some years later Lane's insistence and his attempt to build the giant pumping engines for the city water works all but broke his company. Again, it was not his lack of engineering ability, but that he just did not have a boring mill large enough to machine the huge cylinders.

The winding engines for the cable plant were built by the Hooven, Owens and Rentschler Company of Hamilton, Ohio. There is some confusion as to the exact horsepower of these engines. The *Street Railway Gazette* claims that they were 500 horsepower; Kerper 225 horsepower; the Cincinnati *Enquirer* 800 to 1000 horsepower, and the *U. S. Census Report* of 1890 reported them to be 900 horsepower. Comparing this operation with that of other cable lines 900 horsepower seems to be about right. Also, 73 horsepower was used to move the cars; the rest being consumed by the inertia and friction of the system. This is approximately the correct ratio (10-15) according to the standards of cable railway engineers. As one can readily see, there was an enormous power loss.

There was a slide on Gilbert Avenue hill and a section had to be rebuilt. These difficulties were overcome, and on October 1, 1886, a test run was made. Lane ordered the engines to be slowly turned over. The cable moved at just a few miles per hour.

H. M. Lane handled the grip himself, while a gang of laborers preceded the car with picks and shovels to remove debris that might be on the tracks. The cable was later tested at five and a half miles per hour and finally at the full speed of eight miles per hour. The public opening was eight days later.

Kerper reported to the newspapers on the flawless success of the operation and to the genius of Lane. Later in the year he admitted to some difficulties at a meeting of the American Street Railway Association held at the Burnet House.

At first the problems were minor. The cable insisted on jumping off the driving sheaves. The company experienced difficulty in training competent grip men. The green operators were forever breaking grips and fouling the cable.

A series of accidents of a more serious nature began; culminating in the great wreck of October 2, 1887. It had been a beautiful Indian Summer Sunday, and a large portion of the population was out to enjoy the day. About six o'clock that evening there was a delay in service of about an hour. By seven the cars were again running. The cars going into the city were jammed, and almost all of the traffic was going down the hill. This was a significant factor, as we shall soon see. Car No. 64 picked up a full load; the gripmen whirled the wheel and the car began to descend Gilbert Avenue. On Court Street the grip was released and the brakes were applied but the car proceeded! The gripmen worked frantically with the grip, but it did no good. The conductor came up to help. Still the car sped on grinding around the curves. The passengers became excited, and many of the men jumped off. The inevitable happened. No. 64 plowed into a cable train (a gripcar and trailer) at Sixth Street. The wild trip continued with No. 64 pushing the train ahead. A total of five cars were wrecked and/or thrown off the tracks as the runaway went around the downtown cable loop. Among these were several of the elegant new Pullman cars. The climax was at Fifth and Sycamore Streets. The tracks of the Auburn Avenue cable line had just reached that intersection, and a crossover track was being built. There were open trenches on either side. While this construction was going on, the teams of passing horsecars were detached and led around the trench. The horsecar was then shoved over the crossing by several husky laborers. An Eden Park horsecar was just preparing for this maneuver when the runaway cable cars appeared. Thus, into the trench went the horses, the several cars involved, and their passengers, which consisted mainly of "screaming females."

Remarkably, there were no deaths, but there were many injuries. The incident created a panic. Fully ten thousand persons arrived at the scene and monstrous rumors of calamity were rampant. The wrecked cars provided an opportunity not to be passed up by the newsboys and street urchins, who clambered over these wondrous machines and clanged the car bells to their hearts content.

An investigation was made, and curious causes, for there were a manifold of circumstances, were revealed. The day before the accident a new south cable was installed. New cables had the disagreeable habit of stretching as much as fifty feet on the first day. After a few weeks the cable would settle itself and the normal slack would be taken up by a gravity tension device at the driving station. As mentioned previously on the evening of the wreck, two thirds of the cars were going down grade. Thus, the excess of slack was thrown ahead of the cars. This section of the cable twisted itself into a corkscrew thirty feet long and Car No. 64 was the unfortunate one to first catch up to this snare. Its grip became fouled in the contorted cable, and there was no way for it to free itself.

Lane supposedly altered the tension machinery and a system of callboxes was installed along the line to notify the powerhouse in case of emergency. These precautions by no means meant the end of the accidents, for the cable system is inherently "accident-prone." In order not to drop the cable the grip must be kept on at the curves. At crossovers and certain curves the cable must be dropped and the car would coast through. In either case, full acceleration was maintained.

The lawyer's docket of the company is filled with suits caused by this operating difficulty. Persons were constantly being thrown from their seats or, even worse, over the dashboards onto the street. There is one memorandum in the docket dated June 20, 1894 which might interest the reader, "…. child of four years ran in front of car and was killed. Settlement was made with the father, paying him fifty dollars."

Route 10 produced the majority of the claims, the incline by contrast was strikingly free of accidents. There was one fatality, but this was a track worker and not a passenger. There were accidents, of course, and one of some interest is recalled by Father Alfonse of the Mt. Adams monastery. A children's picnic was to be held at the Highland House one summer. A bakery wagon boarded the incline to be trucked up the hill and deliver pastries to the party. The trip was made unbalanced. There was a mechanical failure and the platform began to roll down the plane gaining momentum. The terrified horses tried to escape but the high fences prevented them. The wagon and the team were horribly crushed, yet, somehow, the driver escaped. The pastries were ruined, and the children were very disappointed.

One of the most bizarre happenings at the Highland was the funeral of its manager. Frank Harff, former operator of the pioneer Lookout House and the manager of the Highland during its best years, died unexpectedly in late October of 1886. Whether it was his thought or not, the idea of a funeral at the Highland was a masterstroke of showmanship. The incline trucks and house draped in black lifted the gloomy assemblage to the hilltop resort. Off to one side of the great center hall, usually the scene of gaiety and good times, lay Harff's coffin. A large crowd assembled

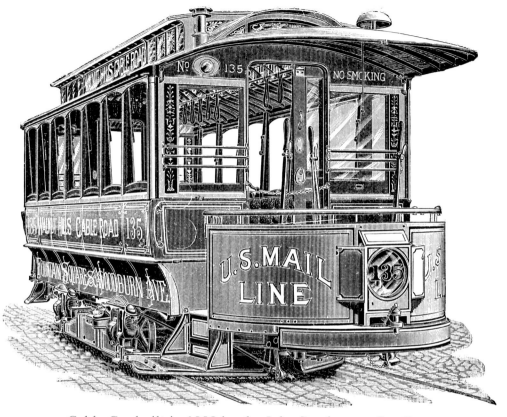

Cable Car built in 1888 by the John Stephenson Car Company
for the Mt. Adams & Eden Park Railway.

Tickets offered transit riders a slight discount when purchased in lots of ten or more.

A Route 10 schedule issued around 1888.

WALNUT HILLS,
Cable Road.

TIME TABLE.

FIRST CAR LEAVES

Turn Table	Fifth and Walnut.
5.30 A. M.	6.00 A. M.

LAST CAR LEAVES

11.20 P. M.	12 P. M.

REGULAR CARS run every Six Minutes.

EXTRA CARS RUN FROM

7 to 9.30 A. M.   3.30 to 7.30 P. M.

Every two-and-one-half minutes.

A SMOKING CAR is attached to *first car that leaves turn table, at 5.30 a. m., and also to last car that leaves at 11.20 p. m.*

Smoking Cars run every 12 minutes.

H. WATKIN, PRINT, 26 LONGWORTH ST.

to view the man who had entertained them for so many years. The services were first given in German and then in English.

The Highland was put up for lease and taken over several months later by P. Rindfieisch and Son.

We now enter into the last episode of the Kerper Road. During the 1870's and 1880's the line rose from a shaky obscure operation to the second largest system in the city. It was the first company to adopt mechanical power and proved to be a spur in urging the Cincinnati Street Railway to improvements. Kerper's voluntary fare reduction to five cents in May 1887 was an innovation. Kerper established the first regular U. S. Mail service via streetcar on July 1, 1887. The experiments with an electric car on Oak Street and with Mr. Silvay's motor, while not successful, were prophetic. Its competition with the "Consolidated" offered material benefits as well as an almost spiritual release to the public. However, the end was in sight. Time was running out for the Little Giant.

Kerper was not content with a static organization. Plans were considered for extending Route 10 to Norwood and building a new line to Hyde Park and even a Price Hill line was mentioned. He did gain permission in 1888 to build a line out Montgomery Pike as far as the C. B. & W. Railroad. At this point his successes stopped. His world seemed to have slipped out from under him. The Street Railway had steadily been buying into the company.

While they did not have large holdings, they did succeed in moving the company's offices in with the Cincinnati Street Railway at the Apollo Building. Then Kerper fell out with John E. Bell, a member of his own Board of Directors. Seemingly, no matter what Kerper proposed, Bell would be in complete opposition.

Frustrated by his own board, he turned again to his friendly jury, the public. Early in the spring of 1889, Kerper carried on one of his typical bombastic, emotional campaigns for his proposed extensions. While he won the popular support, his board would not act. Whether this was a calculated plot or not, it is impossible to ascertain. Without the support of his own directors, there was little else for Kerper to do but resign his office as President. Several months later, on January 21, 1890, he tendered his resignation from the Board of Directors. He stated that he retired to "retain my self-respect."

The *Cincinnati Commercial* lamented the next day, "…. His actual retirement from their services will come with a shock to the public, whom he has so long, so faithfully, so fearlessly, and so progressively served, and with whom he is a decided favorite."

John Kilgour immediately took Kerper's offices and plans were made to cement the consolidation.[28] The extensions Kerper had so untiringly fought for were built, but as properties of the Cincinnati Street Railway.

The remainder of the Little Giant's career was definitely anticlimatical. He directed the city's charities, without pay, for the next year. In the 90's he was Vice-President of the Edison Electric Company.[29] Then he held various offices for several properties of the Cincinnati Traction Company. He died quietly aboard a Pennsylvania Railroad train bound for a pleasure trip to Atlantic City. At the time of his death in 1913, he was a director of the Cincinnati and Columbus Traction Company. At best he was a mere functionary in one corner of the great cosmos of the Ohio Traction Company.[30]

[28] Actual consolidation was accomplished under the Roger's Law July 29, 1896.

[29] By some lucky happenstance, the Gilbert Avenue Cable Railway power-house is still standing. It is one of the last existing links to the pioneer days of city transit. For many years it functioned as home to the Model Laundry. More recently, it was redone (about 1985) as an upscale office complex. The exterior of the building has been restored to its Victorian appearance.

Mt. Adams & Eden Park Railway Oak St. line opened April 20, 1889. *Electric World*, May 25, 1889

And what of the real properties of the Kerper Road? The Eden Park line was electrified in 1890. The incline was rebuilt to accommodate this electric line and after this, the incline house acquired a unique, but quite unintentional form. Surely, its style was meant to be Gothic Revival, yet the shape of the building had become the purest of Gothic forms; that of the cathedral. The simple entrance shed became the atrium; the center hall became a true basilica complete with columns, side aisles and clerestory; the front section became the crossing or transept. The apse was missing, but if you will, the bowl of the valley might fulfill this structural function. Early in February of 1898, the last Gilbert Avenue cable car ran. The Highland House was a victim of the Sunday closing laws in this same period. Ironically, the most primitive of all the Mt. Adams and Eden Park properties, the incline, survived until after WWII.

One may yet walk out from Celestial Street to the edge of Mt. Adams. There, look down the hillside and you will see the stone piers of the plane as they silently crumble into the weeds.

[30] Note: Edmund Kerper lived on for many years in the May Street house built by his father. Edmund died October 1, 1958.

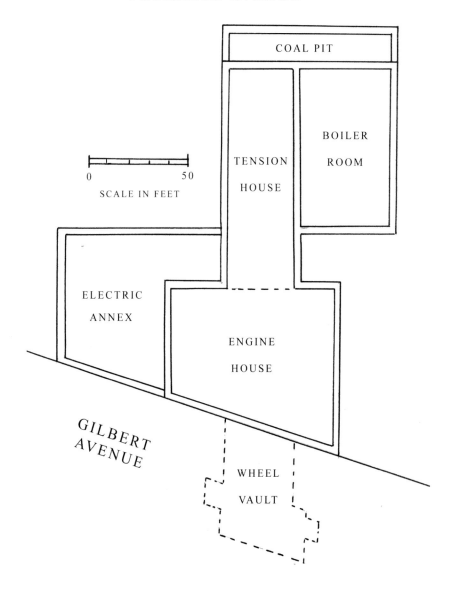

Floor plan of the Gilbert Avenue Power-House.

Chapter 4

The Mt. Adams Incline:
Its History, Operation, and Untimely End

Mention the word incline in Cincinnati and most people think of the Mt. Adams Incline, which is commonly believed to have been Cincinnati's only inclined-plane railway. As we now know the Queen City could once boast of five inclines, six if you count the Price Hill freight plane. But, Mt. Adams became the favorite and the most famous because it was the last in service. Since it ceased operating in 1948, however, the ranks of those citizens who actually rode the rumbling hillside elevator grow smaller each year. The purpose of this essay, then, is to preserve some record of this vanished chapter in local transport history.

Today, Mt. Adams is one of the most fashionable residential areas in the city, but it did not start out that way. It was not even called Mt. Adams; rather, the name was Mt. Ida, after a washerwoman who serviced Fort Washington. Ida Martin is said to have resided in the hollow trunk of a giant sycamore tree near the base of the hill. As the city grew, the trees were felled and hillside quarries left ugly scars in the virgin soil. Some of this damage was hidden by a new owner, Nicholas Longworth, who planted a fine vineyard on the slopes, which he whimsically called The Garden of Eden. The hilltop was renamed in 1843 when former President John Quincy Adams dedicated an astronomical observatory on the site of Holy Cross Monastery. The community that had developed consisted of modest homes and narrow streets, nothing like the stately mansions and grand avenues of Clifton or Mt. Auburn. Yet, it offered a beautiful overlook of the city and river. Immediately behind the little hilltop community was the largest park in the city, Eden Park, newly opened in 1870. Eden Park offered an immediate market for local transportation. Residents might only be working-class folks but they needed to get to and from the basin. After a ten-hour day hanging over a steaming soap vat (or some such occupation), few laborers felt much like hiking up the hillside to get home. Other residents were looking for easy access to the landscaped expanse of parkland. The solution to everybody's needs was an incline railway that would offer rapid transit from the basin to the highlands.

Design, Engineering and Equipment

The corporate history of the Mt. Adams and Eden Park Railway has been told in another essay elsewhere in this volume. Here, we want to focus on the workings of the incline itself, although it will be necessary to retell some of the story of its origins. As with most new enterprises of the kind, the Mt. Adams Incline began with a burst of enthusiasm. Not long after receiving their charter in the summer of 1873, the projectors rushed ahead with construction of the hilltop power station. In May 1874 a local newspaper reported that much of the work was finished. Part of the hilltop had been removed and an excavation cut into the rocky edge, a "cellar" for the hoisting machinery. An adjacent vault had been completed and the boilers were in place. A tall smokestack had also been completed, along with a portion of the head-house, and a cistern had been installed with a capacity of

1,000 barrels of water for the boilers, a precaution should the city water fail. Although the roof was not yet finished and no machinery had been installed, it was clear that everything was moving forward with admirable dispatch.

Chief of the enterprise was Edward M. Shield (1814-79), the proprietor of a local machine shop. Edward's father, Francis, had been a pioneer in the engineering profession, and his sons were carrying on in his tradition. In the case of the Mt. Adams Incline, however, it appears that Shield and associates had moved a little too fast, for they lacked authority to cross several thoroughfares with their track and the city council had demanded that iron bridges be erected over Kilgour, Baum, and Oregon Streets. The council also wanted Shield to include a stop midway up the hill, with necessary platforms and stairways for the use of passengers. Although Shield agreed to both demands, for some reason the council would not enact the necessary legislation for him to proceed. Meanwhile, Shield's health had begun to fail and he had moved to Loveland in hopes that the country air would restore his constitution. The project so bravely started was now foundering.

One of the investors, James E. Mooney, felt certain that new leadership was needed, and he persuaded a young associate to take charge. This was George B. Kerper, who had arrived in Cincinnati in July 1875 and settled into a small house on Ida Street near the construction site. John J. Endres, designer and builder of the Monongahela Incline in Pittsburgh, was hired to take charge of the engineering and in November the newspapers noted that the machinery had been installed. Then, on March 8, 1876 the *Cincinnati Enquirer* reported that the incline had begun operation that morning for invited guests. On Saturday, March 11, it opened to the general public. All in all, the Mt. Adams Incline had cost a little more than $200,000. Highland House was under construction and there was talk of building a narrow-gauge

James E. Mooney

steam-dummy railway from the top station as a belt line through suburban Cincinnati.

Meanwhile the city councilmen, still acting peevishly, had filed a petition against the Mt. Adams Co. in Common Pleas Court for "....specific performance ....." Kerper had failed to build steps and platforms at Baum and Oregon Streets, per an ordinance enacted on August 17, 1874. For his part, Kerper contended that the steps would need to be very high, so high as to pose a danger to passengers. He agreed to begin with the work, but only if the company were relieved from all liability. To add to the potential for accident, one Mike Corbett had opened a saloon next to the site of one of the projected stairways. Good sense finally prevailed and the railway managed to evade the vexatious demands of the councilmen.

While dreams for a narrow-gauge belt-line never materialized, two short horsecar lines were opened soon after the incline began operation. The first was a connection that ran from Lock Street into the city center. The second ran from the top station directly through Eden Park to Grand Street. This was Route 16, and it surely must have been one of the most scenic streetcar lines anywhere in the nation.

A Prefered Stock Certificate issued in May 1883.

Service began in August 1878 with five cars. The grade was so easy that horses could trot all the way. Just a few blocks from the incline, the cars rattled over a bridge spanning a ravine on Ida Street. After a few more blocks of street running, they came to the park grounds and a private right-of-way. The track curved past the Art Museum, passing among trees on grassy slopes. There were vistas of the city, Gilbert Avenue, Mt. Auburn, and Walnut Hills (eventually the line was extended to Gilbert Avenue and on to Walnut Hills). A massive stone bridge over the park's entrance road supported a spindly iron structure, which carried the tracks high above the ground. From this vantage point, passengers could see the waterworks reservoir.

* * *

Within a short time George Kerper, who became known as a tireless advocate of improved public transit, had started to envision a major transformation. In the fall of 1878, he began talking about eliminating the need for a time-consuming transfer between horsecars and the Mt. Adams Incline—that is, about through service from downtown. First, he made tests to see how much power would be required to transport horsecars—passengers and all—up and down the incline on open platforms. There had been just such an operation in Hoboken for several years, and Kerper saw no reason why it could not be emulated in Cincinnati—*provided* you were willing to rebuild and greatly enlarge the existing incline. More timid managers would have protested that the incline railway was only a few years old and that they could not afford to transform a facility that was barely broken in. Think of the investment, think of the stockholders! But Kerper was anything but timid, and he was quite ready to replace a railway barely three years old at whatever cost.

To carry out his grand plan, Kerper hired two young engineers, Henry M. Lane (1854-1929) and Bert L. Baldwin (1858-1942). Both men were employees of the largest machine shop in Cincinnati, the Lane and Bodley Co. Henry Lane was the son of the firm's founder, Philander P. Lane. Their task was not simply to convert the incline into an enormous hillside elevator but to do so with all possible dispatch, for, with the incline out of service, the horsecar connection would be useless. When service was shut down on November 2, 1879, patrons were assured that the inter-ruption would be as brief as possible, but in fact it lasted for almost six months.

Not that the achievement in those six months was not heroic, for this was no mere remodeling job. Both the cellar for machinery and the head-house were substantially

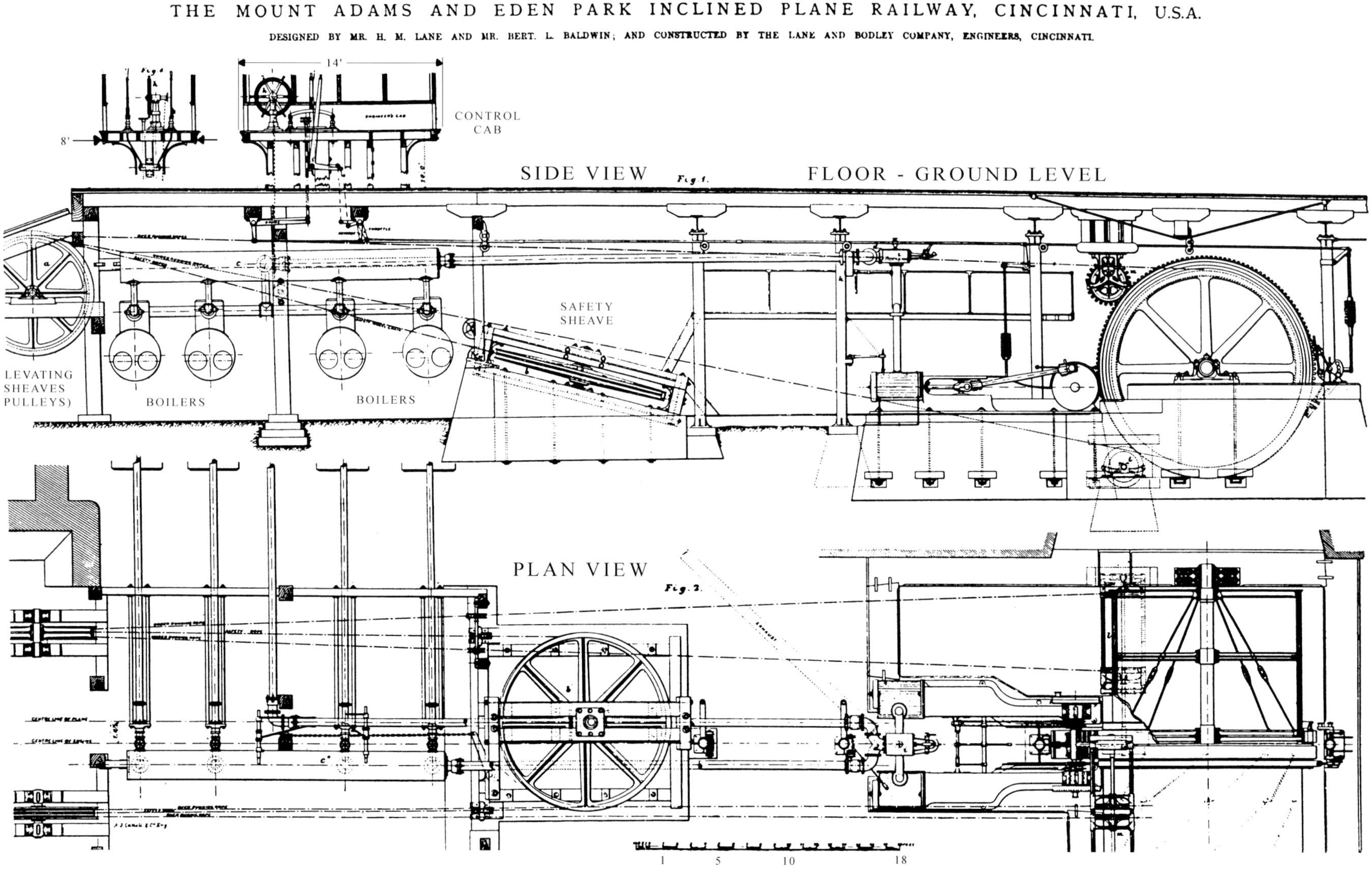

THE MOUNT ADAMS AND EDEN PARK INCLINED PLANE RAILWAY, CINCINNATI, U.S.A.

DESIGNED BY MR. H. M. LANE AND MR. BERT. L. BALDWIN; AND CONSTRUCTED BY THE LANE AND BODLEY COMPANY, ENGINEERS, CINCINNATI.

CONTROL
CAB

SIDE VIEW   FLOOR - GROUND LEVEL

SAFETY
SHEAVE

LEVATING
SHEAVES
PULLEYS)

BOILERS   BOILERS

PLAN VIEW

Fig. 2.

1   5   10   18

The second and enlarged set of winding machinery was installed in 1879 and 1880.
Machinery Drawing from *Engineering*, July 29, 1881

enlarged, and a new broad-gauge track structure was installed that was capable of supporting twenty tons. We know quite a bit about the new machinery because *Engineering* magazine of London ran an article on the Mt. Adams Incline in its issue of July 29, 1881, which included the drawing reproduced on page 74. At the extreme left, one can see the elevating sheaves—cast-iron pulleys 9-1/2 feet in diameter—that guided the cable in and out of the cellar housing the machinery. Nearby is the new chimney and the four boilers, set in separate vaults on the west side of the building; each of these boilers was 42 inches in diameter, 26 feet long, and had two return flues, much like boilers on contemporary river boats. Only two boilers were used at a time. When one pair was down for repairs or cleaning, the second pair was put into service. Just beyond the boilers is seen the safety sheave, mounted on a wooden framework attached to a fieldstone foundation. A single cable wrapped around this huge cast-iron pulley, one end of which attached to each platform or "truck," right and left, and thereby counterbalanced them.

The steam engines were located about 15 feet behind the safety sheave, offset from the centerline of the sheave and the plane itself by 18 inches. These slide-valve engines had 18-by-30-inch cylinders, and the disc cranks were set at 90 degrees from one another with spur gears mounted near the center of the crankshaft. These spur gears engaged wooden teeth on the winding drums, which had cast-iron end and center wheels; the drums themselves were made from oak staves. A threading machine above and below the winding drums laid the cables out in an even pattern. The brakes consisted of wide iron bands with wooden shoes fitting around one end of each winding drum, and were operated by means of foot treadles in the operator's cab, ten feet above the main floor of the top station. Tests proved that the brakes were extremely effective—they could stop the winding machinery dead, even with 100 p.s.i. of steam

pressure and the throttle wide open.

The trucks (platforms) were built up from iron angles, channels, and I-beams, with oak floors. They measured 11 feet wide by 40 feet long and weighed 20 tons each. Each was attached to three separate 1-1/4-inch cables. Mammoth safety catches at the top station were designed to hold the truck back if the engines should ever over-wind, thereby preventing the cables from pulling out of their mountings and allowing the truck to run free down the plane. Had such safety catches been installed on the Main Street Incline, the terrible accident of 1889 would not have happened.

Normal running time was 1-1/2 to 1-3/4 minutes but trips as quick as one minute flat were possible. When a major event was going on at the Highland House, as many as 280 standing pedestrians could be carried on the platforms. Safety was rigorously enforced by the superintendent, who provided each employee with a printed list of questions about every joint, key, bolt, cable, rail—every component of the plane—and expected correct answers. The superintendent took a turn at the controls himself for at least two hours every day to see first-hand how things were working. A system of electric bells and a telephone hookup connected the upper and lower stations, and signals were sent three times before every trip started. A large headlight illuminated the tracks at night. A similar light—this one looking something like a locomotive headlight—is visible in photographs taken at the rear of the top station in the 1880s (page 114).

We should note, finally, that the top station building was remodeled during the 1879-80 construction, because the tracks and truck required a much-enlarged opening, around thirty feet. The new station had a hip roof instead of a dome, and this is the building that survived until the end.

After months of work, the resurrected incline was ready by April 25, 1880. Things were a bit stiff at first and the machinery ran slowly, but other than that, there were no

Engraving of Highland House & Incline circa 1878 showing original top and bottom stations and the Belvedere, an open sided pavilion.

This time, fortunately, the refurbishment could be less extensive. The upper and lower stations required little work; the trucks and the plane itself were fine. But the engines would need upgrading. Bert L. Baldwin was again hired for the design work, and Lane and Bodley took care of the fabrication. The new engines were to be placed to the rear of the winding drums, which meant lengthening the cellar by about 24 feet, and the upper station was extended in the rear to cover the opening. The engines were on the Corliss plan, with rotary rather than slide valves. Such engines used less steam and thus saved fuel and water. The return-flue boilers were replaced with two more conventional fire-tube boilers. A double set of balance (safety) sheaves—one possibly salvaged from the original installation—was installed in a steel frame, a far sturdier arrangement than before. It appears that the winding drums from the 1880 installation were retained, or, if they were new,

problems. On the 26th, hundreds of townspeople came to ride the incline and a sizable crowd gathered at the Highland House to look down on the Ohio River. According to a report in the *Commercial,* it was as muddy as the Tiber. The Kentucky hills gleamed green under the fitful sunshine, but Price Hill was obscured by the smoke from a hundred factories. Indeed, smoke was always part of the Cincinnati scene; it covered the city in a black pall that might have inspired Turner to paint one of his masterpieces. Some visitors were less interested in the view than in the engine room, and this was temporarily opened for public inspection.

By 1890 most street railways were replacing horsecars with electric trolleys, Cincinnati being no exception. That being the case, the Mt. Adams incline was once again obsolescent; the machinery installed just a decade earlier was not powerful enough to handle the greater weight of trolleys.

Incline as rebuilt 1879/80 from a promotional engraving.

they were the same size and in the same position as the 1880 set. Re-using parts of the existing winding machinery naturally saved money and sped the work along. The first rebuilding had required six months; the 1890-91 rebuilding was scheduled for completion in just half that time, beginning October 1, 1890.

As for the streetcar line through Eden Park, putting the heavier trolleys into operation required replacing the old wooden stringers and cap rail with steel T-rail. The Ida Street Bridge - really more a wooden trestle - was strengthened. There was talk of removing the deck on this structure and turning it over

Incline & top station. The large shed-like building at the right was the summer stage, used for theater productions. *Street Railway Journal*, March 1892.

entirely to streetcars, but the public would not hear of it. How would pedestrians enroute to the Park and nearby streets get around the hilltop community? While the incline was shut down, horsecar service continued to Gilbert Avenue where residents of Mr. Adams might catch a cable car into town.

Mechanically, the incline remained largely untouched for the remainder of its service life, the only upgrade of any significance being new trucks in 1936. In the 1930's and '40's, there was talk of replacing the steam engines with electric motors, but it never happened. Historic

preservation's most active allies, as usual, were procrastination and poverty.

Traffic, Operations and Safety

Data concerning traffic on the Mt. Adams Incline is incomplete and scattered. The number of daily trips apparently varied over the years. In his 1932 report on electrification, J.A. Noertker stated that the number was 105. (Of these, five were "unbalanced," that is, one platform had a car while the other was empty.) A fact sheet issued around 1940 by the Cincinnati Street Railway gave the number of daily trips as 114. During the heyday of the Highland House, a popular event such as a Theodore Thomas concert would attract 8,000 people, and it seems certain that most of them got there on the incline. When New York Senator Roscoe Conkling—a Republican stalwart in the 1870s—drew *20,000* to the Highland House, the incline must have coined money for its owners.

Extrapolating from passenger counts for other Cincinnati inclines, it is reasonable to assume that Mt. Adams transported about one million passengers per year for most of its history. (From the 1890 census, we definitely know that the Eden Park line carried more than 1.2 million passengers that year.) In December 1947 a local newspaper indicated that weekday ridership was 5,000 passengers, with 8,000 on Sundays—an indication that the incline was even then a tourist attraction. Based on these numbers, the annual passenger count would be around 1,971,000. At ten cents a head that looks like a lot of revenue but of course just about all riders paid regular streetcar fares credited to the Zoo—Eden streetcar line. Revenue earned separately by the incline was modest. Foot passengers generated $6,777 in fares in 1929, $5,137 in 1932. In 1918 the city set a rate of 2-1/2 cents for foot passengers, and this had apparently doubled by 1932.

Freight—wagons at first and later motor trucks—brought in some revenue as well. Before the advent of the gasoline engine a few of the Cincinnati inclines, especially Bellevue and Price Hill, did rather well hauling loaded wagons to the top of the hill. But this was not true of the Mt. Adams incline. In 1902-03, when teams and wagons monopolized the goods traffic, Mt. Adams collected only $893, according to a statement reproduced in Wagner and Wright's incline booklet. We suspect that there were two reasons for this: Gilbert Avenue offered a fairly easy grade for horse-drawn wagons and Mt. Adams was too small a community to generate much freight traffic.

Conversely, foot-passenger traffic on the Mt. Adams Incline was far stronger than on the other inclines operated by the Cincinnati Traction Company. In the 1902-03 accounting, foot passengers brought in just over $5,000, which represents a lot of 2-1/2 cent fares and a steady parade of workers and shoppers who preferred to hoof it downtown, at least part way, to save a nickel a day. Mt. Adams was a thrifty community of working-class citizens who watched their pennies and who would have been astonished by free-spending residents of the present day, who would not stop to

Incline operator Foster G. Carroll. His left hand rests on the throttle lever. The coil pipe on the right side is a steam radiator. *The Cincinnati Post*, March 26, 1948.

pick up a penny if the sidewalk were covered with them. The foot-passenger trade held up well until the incline's last days, with 1947 revenues amounting to $8,407.05, according to a note in *Enquirer of* May 10, 1948.

* * *

During the 1950s, I gathered information on the operation of the incline from conversations with three former employees: Forrest Himes, superintendent of buildings and inclines for the Street Railway starting in the 1920s; Charles Schnittger, who worked as a fireman in the engine room for many years; and Foster G. Carroll, who was an operator during the incline's last years. Carroll started as an operator at Mt. Adams in 1932. He died on December 13, 1977 at the age of 74. Additional details were found in a *Cincinnati Post* article for August 8, 1902. Service began at 5:30 a.m. and ended at 12:45 a.m. During the downtime, the fireman (who doubled as a watchman) kept a small fire under the boiler, and each morning he would stoke up this fire to raise a full head of steam for the trial run before the first car arrived. The engineer climbed under the truck at the top station and rode precariously down to the bottom. Because the nighttime coolness caused the cables to shrink, it was necessary to adjust their length at the bottom station for a proper landing. This was done through adjusting screws as shown in plate 5 and the photo to the right. Later in the day he would make another trip to shorten the cables, which the heat of the sun would have caused to expand. The seldom-used safety brake was tested during the first run each morning.

Once regular service began, operators were instructed to run balanced trips— that is to have a car on each platform if at all possible. Sometimes this was not possible, however, when tie-ups would delay arrivals either from the park or city end of the line. If one car was on board and a second

Cable adjusters under one of the new trucks 1936. The three adjuster levers and rachets are visable near the center of this view

Looking down the plane from the operator's cab.

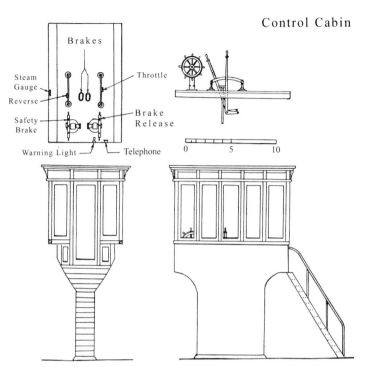

Control Cabin

Brakes

Steam Gauge
Reverse

Throttle

Safety Brake

Brake Release

Warning Light

Telephone

0   5   10

Drawing above details the positions of the operators controls

Looking up at the operators cab.

car was not sighted after waiting three minutes, an unbalanced trip was run. Although this could be done safely, it put a greater strain on the winding machinery and the brakes, and, of course, on the nerves of the operator. In the days of four-wheel streetcars more trips were necessary and the incline ran faster to make a trip in just 90 seconds. In 1921 larger eight-wheel cars were introduced on the Zoo-Eden Line, and by 1932 the pace was greatly slowed, to 2-1/2 minutes, both in the interest of safety and of preventing wear and tear on the aging machinery and track structure.

The operator was the central figure amongst the employees of the incline. While at work, he stood inside a rectangular control cab that was ten feet above the main floor of the top station, supported by a slender base rising up from between the two streetcar tracks. The cab and controls installed in 1880 apparently survived until the end. There was a narrow iron stairway (fourteen steps) up to the rear of the cab. Although he could see in all directions—the cab was surrounded by glass windows—the operator usually gazed straight ahead, keeping the tracks in clear focus. The bottom portion of the cab was cut back on an angle to offer greater clearance as larger cars were introduced over the years.

The controls were simple. The reverse lever was on

the right-hand side, the throttle on the left. Because the quadrants were not notched, the controls were at the instant command of the operator. Two foot pedals worked the brakes on the winding drums. This was a manual system, which required that the operator put all his weight on the pedals. The surface area of the brakes was very generous, however, and so the system worked well. The backup brake system, on the balance sheaves, was operated by a wind-up wheel—the design like a ship's steering wheel—on the right side. The left-hand wheel released the automatic brake. Rods and cables connecting the levers and wheels to machinery below passed down through the cab's supporting column. A telephone, signal bell, and red warning light were mounted on the left side of the cab's front wall. The warning light was actuated by a switch in the engine room. If a problem developed down below, the operator could be instantly alerted by the engineer. A steam gauge was placed at eye level on the right side of the cab, and operators were instructed not to attempt an unbalanced lift if steam pressure was less than 90 p.s.i.

Operating the incline was much like running a steam locomotive and much depended on the skill of the man at the throttle. Training and experience were surely important but a fine sense of speed and timing was necessary as well. In 1902 an operator named Chris Hollinger remarked that "the speed of the trucks is regulated by the operator's eye and the sound of the running cables." The ritual of operation was as follows: First the gateman at the bottom station notified the operator that the car was on the truck and the gate was closed by ringing two bells. (The top gateman gave the operator the same signal when the car was successfully loaded on the top truck.) The bottom gateman then rang four bells, which indicated that all was ready; the gates would not be opened, even for a sprinting foot passenger, under any circumstances. The operator rang four bells to each

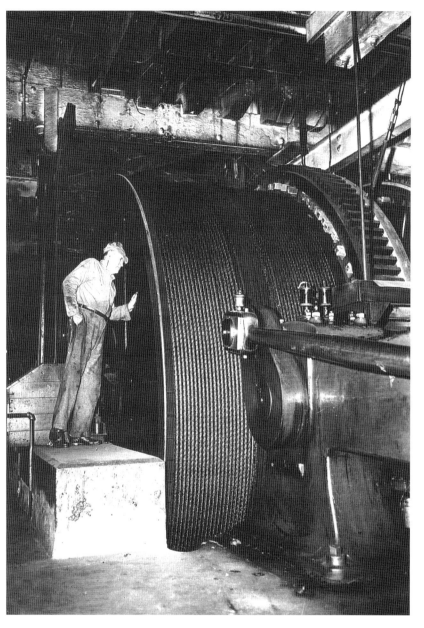

Drury Knox, incline engineer, inspecting one of the winding drums. The cranks of one of the steam engines is visible in the foreground. *Cincinnati Post* photo.

gateman (if there were any questions, the telephone was used), reversed the engines, and released the safety catch on the upper truck. He then gently opened the throttle. The plane was now in operation, with speed controlled by braking the descending truck. When the ascending truck was within 280 feet of the top station, the throttle was closed; then slowly reopened. The engines were put in reverse and with the aid of the brake a smooth landing was made.

The engineer had the second-highest level of responsibility. No steam plant of any size could be operated in the city without a licensed stationary engineer and that regulation surely covered the Mt. Adams Incline. The engineer made adjustments and repairs on a daily basis. Always he watched but, more, he smelled and listened. What was that smell: a hot bearing? Sounds that would mean nothing to the ordinary person would set an engineer into motion, walking around, looking and listening. An unfamiliar sound was often a signal that something was running amiss.

These fellows could often avert a breakdown by catching a problem when it was just beginning. The following story is illustrative. One evening in the 1930s the engineer on duty noticed a slight wobble in one of the giant sheave wheels, and he immediately notified the superintendent, Mr. Himes. The repair crew was called and, as soon as the last car was trucked, the safety rig was taken down. The bottom bearing of one of the safety sheave shafts was completely worn out! For a moment it appeared as though all operations would need to cease for some time, possibly forever. Himes showed himself to be a good Yankee mechanic, however, and he sent the crew hurrying to the abandoned Elm Street Incline. Elm Street had identical machinery, designed by Bert Baldwin—the only difference being that the engines were Buckeyes. A bearing was cannibalized and hurried back to Mt. Adams. Car jacks and

Safety sheaves being inspected in the engine room. Note the large bearings at the center of each sheave. The center or safety cable wrapped around these two wheels. We are looking toward the south in this view.

timbers were put to good use in blocking up the sheave. The bearing was replaced. All was in good order and the plane opened the next morning as though nothing had happened.

A maintenance man inspected the trestle and made small repairs on a daily basis. He would also do jobs as needed around the top and bottom stations. Only the most skilled carpenter was up to repairing the trestlework and he would need help when it came to handling large timbers. The 24-foot ties were replaced at night during the shutdown hours, working by the light of lanterns.

According to J. A. Noertker, an engineer employed by the Cincinnati Street Railway, total employment on the incline was fourteen men: three engineers, three operators, three firemen, one oiler, and four gatemen. A full crew consisted of an operator, a fireman, an engineer and two gatemen. Operations were carried on seven days a week, 19 to 20 hours a day, hence we must be speaking of 10-hour shifts and *5-1/2* to 6 day weeks. Note that Noertker made no mention of the carpenter/maintenance man but Forrest Himes definitely spoke of such an employee during our conversations. Perhaps oiler was another job title for the fourteenth man, and the fact that he worked only one shift is of interest. Here, as with many other questions about the Mt. Adams Incline, there seems to be no way to arrive at a definitive answer.

A timid traveler must have had distinct misgivings when first confronted with that long, steep track that seemed to go straight down. How safe is this thing? Am I really ready to trust my life to this bizarre pile of brick, lumber, and cast iron? Whatever answer that individual may have

Looking down hill. The grade was less steep than it appears.

come up with, millions of Cincinnatians rode the incline over the years without much concern. And for good reason. No passenger was ever killed or even seriously injured on the Mt. Adams Incline during all its seventy-two years of service. Oh, surely, there were some bumps and thumps during all of those thousands of trips. Even the best operator must have made a hard landing from time to time. Indeed, we can report one such incident that occurred just at the time the plane started to handle larger double-truck streetcars. Late in June 1921 there was an extra hard landing at Lock Street, not long after the trucks had been lengthened. This caused enough excitement for the city to close the incline for a full week. After repeated inspections turned up no defects, however, service was resumed.

The record for employee safety, on the other hand, was less than perfect; three workmen having died during the first twenty-five years of operation. The *Commercial* for September 12, 1883, told the gruesome story of James Covalt, a sixty-two year-old handy man who did work around the Highland House and the incline. Covalt was working out on the plane about halfway up, and as a car approached, he laid down in the center of the track thinking the car would pass over him. Unfortunately, there was only four inches of clearance and he was dragged a short distance before the power could be shut down. His body badly mangled and his head severed, his remains were gathered in a blanket and removed for burial. Somehow, the death of a workman was more acceptable than the loss of a passenger would have been. It was just a hazard of the job.

Of course safety was of primary importance for the

obvious reason that the incline carried passengers and was perceived as a dangerous means of transport. Moreover, because of its size and prominent hillside location, it could be seen from many points in and around the city. Each day people would look over and wonder when that thing was going to crash. The builders and managers of the incline were determined that day would never come, and they did all they could to make it as safe as was humanly possible.

First, everything was built on a massive scale—the heavier, the better. The weighty and oversized machinery insured an added measure of strength and a long service life. The basic design of a balanced incline plane—two trucks tied together by a common cable—was in itself a built-in safety factor. Two draft or haulage cables were used for each platform. The notion being if one failed the second would hold fast. These cables were 1-1/4 inches in diameter, while the safety or balance cable was 1-3/8 inches. The cables had a combined strength of 224 tons,

Photo shows teeth of drum gearing on the left. Counter weights for the Lilly Control are on the right.

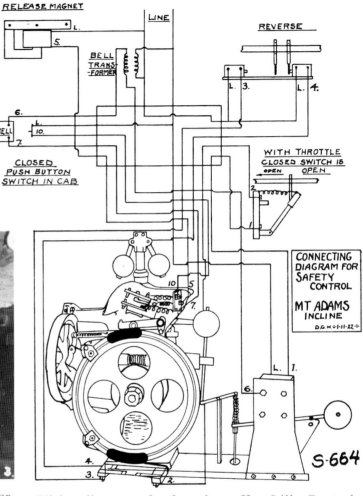
Wiring diagram of safety shut-off or Lilly Control.

a safety factor of four, and they were inspected monthly by an employee of the Otis Elevator Company.

Some time before 1883, safety hooks or latches were installed at the top station to hold the trucks fast should the

cables fail or be pulled loose. As a backup, there was a separate steam shut-off. It was simple and cheap but effective, a butterfly valve in the main steamline leading from the boilers to the engines. This was held open by a cable running up to the operator's cab, its looped end being slipped

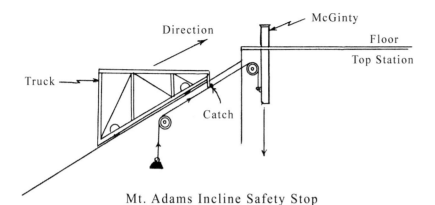

Mt. Adams Incline Safety Stop

Top station details of the elevating wheels; the small cable between the first and second wheel works the McGinty. Photo dates after the abandonment in 1948. Note the wooden barracade across the tracks in the upper left.

over a peg. If the operator experienced any problems with the throttle, all he needed to do was pull the cable off its peg and steam pressure would instantly slam the butterfly valve shut.

An automatic brake was installed in 1920-21. Also called a Lilly Control, this was a standard device used on mine hoisting machinery, patented by William J. Lilly of Butte, Montana, on September 2, 1919. When the ascending truck was within 280 feet of the top station, a warning bell would sound. If the operator failed to reduce the speed of the truck, the automatic brake took over. The heart of the Lilly Control was in a box located at the east end of the main shaft of the winding drums. A centrifugal governor was actuated by the shaft's rotation. If the speed were excessive, the governor would open a switch cutting off the current and breaking the magnetic field. With its field broken, a solenoid would allow a set of half-ton counterweights to fall. By means of a cable and lever arrangement, the force of the falling weights would set the service brakes and slam the throttle shut. This would result in a very quick stop indeed. If the operator lost control of the plane for any reason, he could set the Lilly Control by pushing a button; in effect, it was a "deadman." The control rarely took over, but, on those occasions when it did, passengers were greatly unnerved and operators were suspended if this occurred too often.

The car "stops" were steel I-beams that stood about 36 inches above the pavement in their up or stop position; when in the open or pass position, they dropped to street level. There were six of them, one for both tracks at the top and bottom stations, and one for each truck. These were centered in the track and together served the useful purpose of preventing a car from rolling out of the top station, or into a pit at the bottom station, or off one of the trucks. The stops were referred to by the incline's employees as the "McGinty." It seems there was an old sea chanty about McGinty popping above the waves; the jocular antics of the salty McGinty being very similar to the bobbing action of the car stops. The McGinty's normal position was up, being counterbalanced. The ascending truck, for example, would grapple the "catch" pulling the cable forward, causing the McGinty to "sink out of sight under the waves," or drop to the down position. (See p. 85 for diagram.)

On Ida Street just outside the top station, the streetcar tracks merged and then diverged again so that cars could align with the right or left truck, whichever happened to be waiting at the time. The switch was manual, meaning that the motorman would have to stop his car and climb down to throw it. He was now reminded that the incline was dead ahead and that he had best choose the correct track. It became common practice, however, for the gateman to walk back and line up the switch. One Sunday afternoon, for no certain reason, the gateman failed to throw the switch and the preoccupied motorman rolled his car on to the wrong track. Instead of easing onto the waiting truck (which was lined up at the opposite track), he slammed into the McGinty. The McGinty stood fast.

The Decline and Fall

The postwar years were good times for the United States. The economy boomed and business and industry prospered. But the transit industry did not share in this prosperity. Patronage slumped as Americans turned more and more to private automobiles. Cutbacks and modernization were the order of the day around the Cincinnati Street Railway. Streetcars were seen as unwieldy road hogs that slowed down traffic, and the public and the city government seemed agreed on a policy of early retirement for this mode of transit. At the same time, many Cincinnatians regarded the Mt. Adams Incline as something of a civic ornament, and felt confident that the managers of the Street Railway—especially old-timers such as Walter Draper—shared that feeling. Even so, management was under great pressure to modernize and economize. C.S.R. was a private corporation and its stockholders expected

dividends. The incline might be a popular tourist attraction but it was hardly a moneymaker. It required a fair-sized crew to run it and labor costs were climbing.

On top of that, the physical plant needed constant maintenance. The winding machinery remained serviceable even though it was more than fifty years old, but the steam plant was obsolete. An electric drive would reduce operating costs, but then such a sizable investment in new trolleys or motorbuses seemed far more attractive. The inclined plane itself was a ramshackle wreck of wobbly stone piers and aging timbers. Sure, one could patch and hope, but would not it really be preferable to replace all this with proper steelwork?

Most Cincinnatians, even if they perceived these problems, seemed content in the belief that the incline would go on forever. These same trusting folks no doubt also believed that the Tyler Davidson fountain would remain where it belonged on Fountain Square right in the middle of Fifth Street. The explosion and sinking of the *Island Queen* in 1947 might have been taken as an omen that bad things were going to happen to some other great old relics. The days of wine and roses were about over. The original Fountain Square was demolished, the early public landing was ripped out and dumped—and the Mt. Adams Incline was abandoned. Cincinnati entered the Dark Age of the Master Plan, Fort Washington Way, and a pair of horrid sports arenas. All of these elephantine projects proved extraordinarily expensive and of dubious benefit.

* * *

In July 1947, the Eden Park entrance bridge was condemned for streetcar service. This signaled the beginning of the end for the Mt. Adams Incline, which carried its last streetcar, No. 2446, up the hill at 12:46 a.m. on July *25,* 1947. Led by its new president, Max J. Palm, Jr., the Park Board was not content to be rid of the streetcars; the board also declared the McLaughlin' s stone arch bridge a hazard and ordered it demolished (The supposedly crumbling structure proved so hardy that it had to be dynamited). The beautiful streetcar ride through Eden Park was thus ended by the prophets of Progress. The Street Railway substituted buses on the Zoo-Eden line, sending them up and down the incline, at least for a time. But soon enough, insurance inspectors declared the structure to be unsafe. The last bus was trucked up the hill on April 16,1948, and a sign put up saying **'Closed for Repairs'.** This was greeted with proper skepticism and, of course, the incline never ran again.

The public was clearly upset. This was not just any old piece of iron or some unwanted has-been. This was our incline and, even if we did not ride it very often, we wanted it to be there. There were petitions and letters to the editor. All told, the three Cincinnati newspapers published some forty editorials, all of them supportive of reopening the Mt. Adams plane. The *Times Star* was particularly passionate in its editorials calling for restoration, perhaps because the incline was within easy view of that paper's offices. Some eloquent prose was produced. One editorial remarked that the incline was really not "needed" any more than the zoo or the parks are needed, but that a city that limits itself to the bare necessities is a city without character. The incline was said to represent something priceless in the life of the city, something irreplaceable. Perhaps the best argument was that a community is only as big as its traditions; size and wealth mean nothing if a soul is lacking.

This was heavy rhetoric and the politicians naturally ran for cover. 'Ordered' to make repairs, the company pleaded poverty and passed the problem back to the city. In October 1948, Mayor Albert D. Cash stated flatly he was "opposed to saddling the taxpayers with this much expense." The sums involved in making repairs were actually fairly small, $125,000 or maybe $150,000. True, annual operating losses of around $50,000 could be expected, but if this debate had taken place a decade or two later, it is likely that the city would have accepted these as a good investment in terms of tourism and public pride. (Pittsburgh recently spent three million dollars to redo the Monongahela Incline without much comment.) But in the late 1940s many of our younger civic leaders saw historic monuments merely as Victorian monstrosities. The sooner they could be eliminated, the better. One must also consider that historic preservation did not command the respect or political clout it commands today, particularly not in cities. Yes, old houses and monuments were sometimes preserved but not in any systematic manner. There were not the advocacy groups watching over historic properties that there are today.

A stronger indication of public interest might have induced public officials to act more sympathetically. Politicians will support almost any project they feel is popular, but an apathetic public only confirms that no action is called for. The Chamber of Commerce might have pushed vigorously to save the incline as a tourist attraction, but again, it was just a decade or two too early for this kind of thinking. Progress and modernity were the watchwords, at least in Cincinnati. Matters were handled differently in San Francisco in 1947 after the mayor had made it clear that the cable cars must go. An aroused citizenry emphatically disagreed and voted more than three-to-one to save the antique system. There was (and is) no question about the cable cars being inefficient and costly to operate. Yet, they remain a major attraction in a city notable for its efforts to save important elements of the past. Still, Cincinnati has no incline.

* * *

In 1950 the City Council voted to relieve the Street Railway of any obligation to repair the incline. Developers

Rear view of top station, about a year after operations ceased.

site was eventually paved for a parking lot.

The bottom station fared differently. It was purchased by a local resident on Lock Street, and there it remained. In June 1963, I visited Lock Street to take measurements and complete a set of drawings I had begun in 1957, reproduced here as Plates 1 through 8. During this visit, Calvin Williams, the owner of the building, stopped to chat saying that he hoped to find a way to preserve the structure - the last intact remnant of the incline. But Calvin's plans were not shared by the highway department. About nine years later, Route 471 came through the area and wiped out the station, all of Lock Street and a large part of Mt. Adams hillside. Just how much of Cincinnati's early history was swept away by this mammoth earth-moving project would be difficult to say, but it was no doubt considerable.

During a more recent visit, in June 1999, it appeared to me that the old incline right-of-way remains intact. Through the weeds I could see the ruins of some of the stone piers. It is no wonder that new housing has not sprung up on this land, even considering the fashionable nature of the Mt. Adams. A landslide in the late 1970s led to the demolition of many houses on Baum and Kilgour Streets. A large and very expensive retaining wall was finished in 1982. But, even this $2.5 million protective measure has prompted little new construction. And may there never be. It is my personal hope that the abandoned pathway be allowed to slumber and that we will hear of no more schemes for putting up tacky skylifts or aerial cableways that would diminish, rather than enhance, the memory of the Mt. Adams incline.

then bought the property intending to build a deluxe high-rise apartment building on the former site of the Highland House, just to the east of the incline's top station. The demand for scrap iron during the Korean War prompted the new owners to salvage the machinery and rail. A permit to scrap was issued in February 1952, and soon the acetylene torches were cutting up 500 tons of old iron and steel. The hillside plane was demolished at the same time, with all work being finished by April. But, the two stations remained standing. The gutted top station became a magnet for local youngsters and, with the main floor partially ripped out in order to remove the machinery, it was a serious hazard. City Inspectors had little choice but to condemn the whole structure. It was torn down in the spring of 1954, and the

Top station site after demolition , 1954c. The piers of the safety sheaves can be seen in the foreground. The basement cavity was filled in and paved over for a parking lot. No marker stands to proclaim the site of Cincinnati's famous Mt. Adams Incline. *Cincinnati Post* photo.

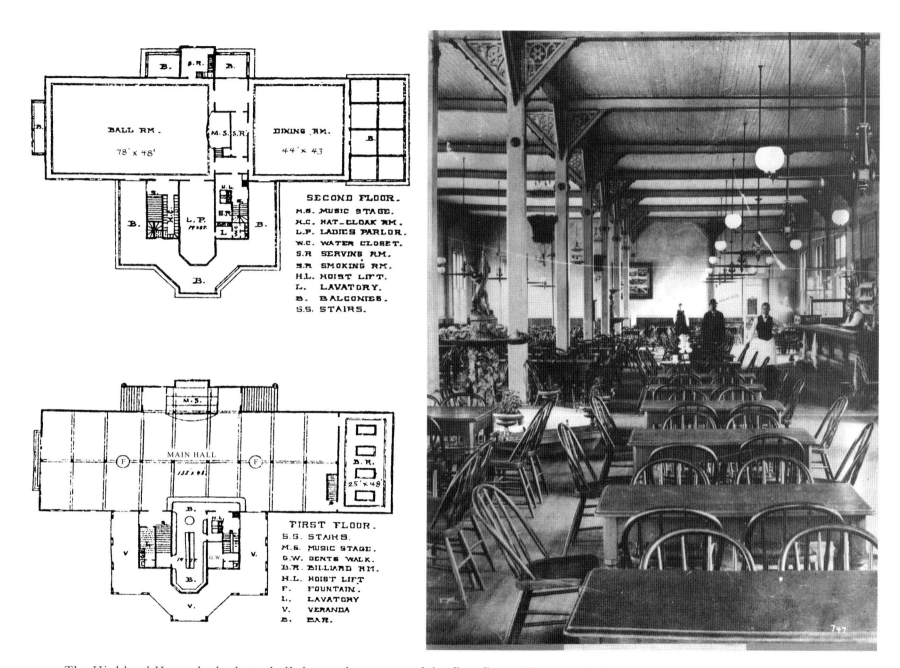

SECOND FLOOR.

BALL RM.
78' x 48'

DINING RM.
44' x 43

M.S. MUSIC STAGE.
H.C. HAT-CLOAK RM.
L.P. LADIES PARLOR.
W.C. WATER CLOSET.
S.R. SERVING RM.
S.R. SMOKING RM.
H.L. HOIST LIFT.
L. LAVATORY.
B. BALCONIES.
S.S. STAIRS.

FIRST FLOOR.

MAIN HALL
135' x 48'

B.R.
25' x 48'

S.S. STAIRS.
M.S. MUSIC STAGE.
G.W. GENTS WALK.
B.R. BILLIARD RM.
H.L. HOIST LIFT
F. FOUNTAIN.
L. LAVATORY
V. VERANDA
B. BAR.

The Highland House had a large hall that took up most of the first floor. The second floor boasted spacious dining and ball rooms. The photograph shows the Main Hall with a bar on the right side and the fountains on the left or north side.

'Welcome to the Land of Pleasant Living'
A Tour Around Highland House

For all of the fanciful legends and romantic tales associated with this resort, the building was a fairly cheap, wooden structure much on the order of a small summer hotel. It was pepped up with a couple of towers and a multitude of gingerbread verandas and balconies. The main rectangle measured around 160 feet by 50 feet. The front bay was a two-story structure of 25 by 50 feet. The major part of the first floor was devoted to the 'main hall', which was sometimes called the beer hall. This large space measured 135 x 48 feet and featured a plentitude of tables and chairs for 2000 patrons. It had two interior bronze fountains and a large bar on the south side. The music stand was on the north side of the 'main hall'. At the far east side was a billiard room which had floor space for four tables.

There was a second bar in the forward bay. Stairways, lavatories, and an elevator shaft were worked into the south center portion of the first floor. The elevator went up into the front tower. Around the upper section of the tower was a balcony that offered a great view of the city. Those into fitness were welcome to climb the stairs.

The second floor was more cut up than the main floor. It was also stepped back around 25 feet at the east end. The restaurant on the east side measured 44 by 48 feet. A dance hall, sometimes more grandly referred to as the 'Ball Room', occupied the west side of the second floor. A music stand was at the center end of the ballroom. A good size ladies' parlor was placed in the front bay. There were stairways, water closets, and a hat and cloakroom, plus a smoking room on this floor.

The basement of the Highland House was home to a kitchen and laundry facility measuring 65 by 24 feet. An adjacent bowling

George W. Rapp, architect of the Highland House. *Industries of Cincinnati* 1886.

alley of about the same size had four lanes, each 70 feet long. The lower level also contained beer vaults and wine storage rooms. The entire building was heated by steam and cost over $50,000 to build.

In 1877, a summer pavilion called the Belvedere was erected to the east side of the hilltop resort. It was a high and open structure, 75 x 150 feet with a stone floor. It seated 7000 people and was sometimes used for dancing, balls, roller-skating and even public picnics. The Belvedere had a large stage done in a grotto style and was outfitted with scenery and footlights. The stage was at the north end.

Sometime later, perhaps as late as 1890, a second and smaller summer theater was erected next to the incline powerhouse. It was actually built next to the trestle and was so high it stood in front of the east segment of the top station building. It was a crude shed-like structure. An engraving published in the March 1892 *Street Railway Journal* (see p. 77), shows one of the best illustrations of this clumsy box of a building. The summer stage had scenery and footlights as well. We suspect its completion was intended to add a new attraction to the Highland House facility during its declining years. With the resort's demise in 1895, the summer stage apparently fell to the wreckers' hammer. Yet, some vestige of this structure, much reduced, is visible in the Detroit Publishing Company's 1906 photograph, reproduced on page 16. We suspect the shed was used for a repair shop until it was replaced by the brick structure erected in 1912.

The grounds were something to behold as well. There were statues in stone, bronze, iron and marble. Fountains and lush flowerbeds completed the effect.

(This account is based on information presented in *The American Architect*, March 2, 1878, the *Cincinnati Gazette*, December 20, 1876 and the Sanborn Fire Insurance map of 1891.)

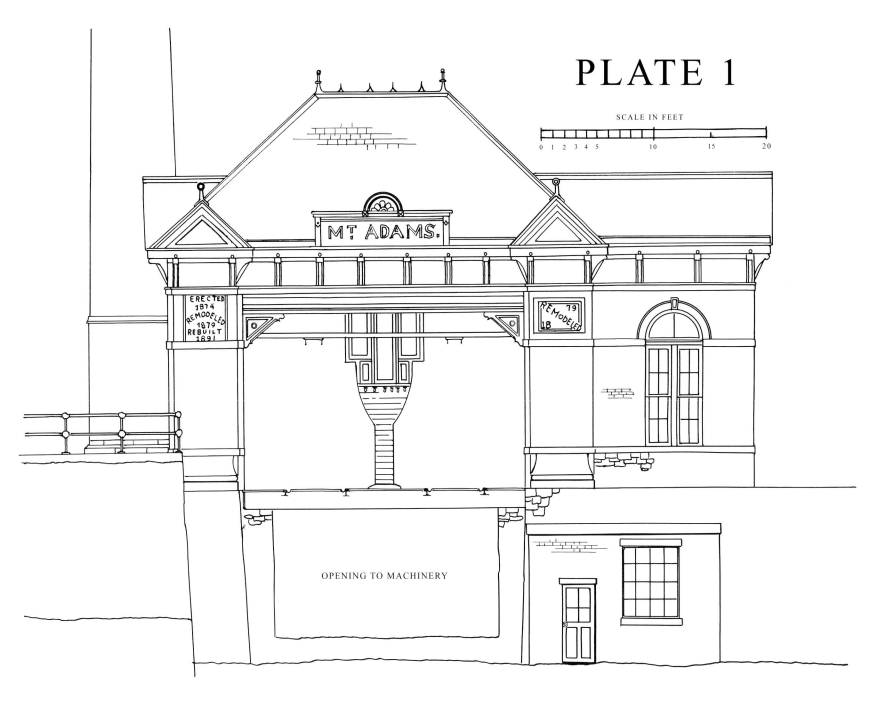

PLATE 1

SCALE IN FEET

0 1 2 3 4 5   10   15   20

M͟T ADAMS.

ERECTED
1874
REMODELED
1879
REBUILT
1891

REMODELED 79
18

OPENING TO MACHINERY

Plate 1 - Front Elevation of the Top Station

This drawing is a reconstruction based on measurements taken after the building had been demolished in 1954. The lower sections of the sidewalls were standing at the time, so I was able to obtain some crucial measurements. Other dimensions and details were scaled from photographs. The main floor of the structure was at ground level. The facade of the building remained largely unaltered after the 1880 rebuilding. It was a typical Victorian commercial structure built of brick and stone. The roof and floor were of timber construction reinforced with truss rods. The roof was covered with slate — the flashing was tin or galvanized sheet metal. The cornices and decorative elements, such as the tables "erected in 1874" and so on, were made from galvanized sheet metal. The letters were individually fabricated and stood out in relief. They were painted a cream color and highlighted in black. Most visitors might have assumed all of this was carved wood or stone. I salvaged the numerals for 1879 at the time of the demolition and gave these to the Cincinnati Historical Society in 1977.

The inclined plane structure has been omitted in this drawing and the space below the main floor labeled "opening to machinery" was actually partially boarded up to keep out the weather. Passages for the elevating sheaves and cables were cut into this partition. Glass window sashes were incorporated into the partition wherever possible to admit natural light into the dark cavern of the machinery room. The control cab can be seen in the center of the main opening. The operator stood here to manage the throttle and brakes. His station was elevated ten feet above the main floor and was surrounded by large windows to offer the operator good visibility. Notice that the sides of the operator's cab were cut away to offer clearance as larger streetcars were introduced over the years.

To the left of the building can be seen a platform which forms a roof for the coal cellar below. An iron pipe handrail was in place for the security of visitors. This platform offered a fine view of the city below. The large brick chimney was on the same side of the building, but was well back from the edge of the hillside. Contemporary engravings indicate that a similar chimney stood on the east side of the top station when the incline first opened in 1876. A new and larger chimney was erected on the west side during the 1879-1880 reconstruction.

The small brick room on the east side at the basement level was erected in 1912. It served as a workshop for minor repairs to the machinery. It had access to the basement machinery room through the front wall of the lower level. Note the comparatively modern steel casement style of window in the front wall.

This drawing was one of seven completed by the author between 1956 and 1958. A set of these plans was given to the Cincinnati Historical Society at this time and so was available to the public. Several of the drawings were reproduced in Wagner and Wrights' Booklet *Cincinnati Streetcars No. 2: The Inclines; 1968.* The drawings were, for some reason, incorrectly credited to someone else, even though they are clearly copies of my work.

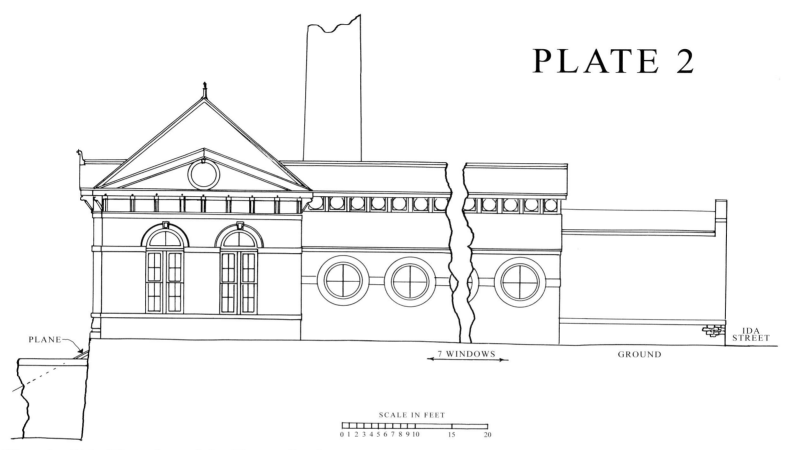

PLANE

7 WINDOWS

GROUND

IDA
STREET

SCALE IN FEET

0 1 2 3 4 5 6 7 8 9 10   15   20

Plate 2 - Side Elevation of the Upper Station

The structure of the upper station is shown as it appeared from 1891 through 1948. It was a long building, around 128 feet, built in three sections. The front section was built in 1879-1880 to replace the original portion that featured a large dome and side wings to service the fixed cab cars. The new front section was made wider to accommodate the passage of the horse cars and later, electric streetcars. The center part of the building, with seven round windows per side, was retained from the original structure. It has a clerestory roof and once featured a rear portal with

the words "Eden Park Railway" in raised galvanized iron letters - see pg. 114. When new engines were installed in the 1891 rebuilding, more machinery space was needed and so the basement was lengthened by 24 feet. A plain brick structure was added on to cover the elongated basement. It pushed the building out to meet the intersection formed by Ida and Celestrial Streets. A portion of the repair shed is shown at the extreme left side of Plate 2. It had three casement windows in the east wall and a door in the west wall that allowed access to the underside of the incline structure and the elevating wheels.

PLATE 3

Plate 3 - Rear Elevation Top Station

EXHAUST PIPE

Coal Track

SCALE IN FEET

0 1 2 3 4 5 6 7 8 9 10

J. H. WHITE 1956

The centerline of the top station was directly in line with Ida Street. A visitor could look directly through the building in a southerly direction to the city and river. Today this area is an asphalt parking lot situated between the Rookwood Pottery and the Highland Towers apartment building. This view is essentially self-explanatory but we should comment on a few details. The small brick addition on the West Side of the building was the last structural addition to the top station, according to Mr. Himes, the former superintendent. He could not recall the date at the time of our conversation in the 1950's, but it was probably in the 1920's. This low structure housed water-softening apparatus used to treat the boiler water. The exhaust pipe for engines and feed water pumps was placed at this location as well.

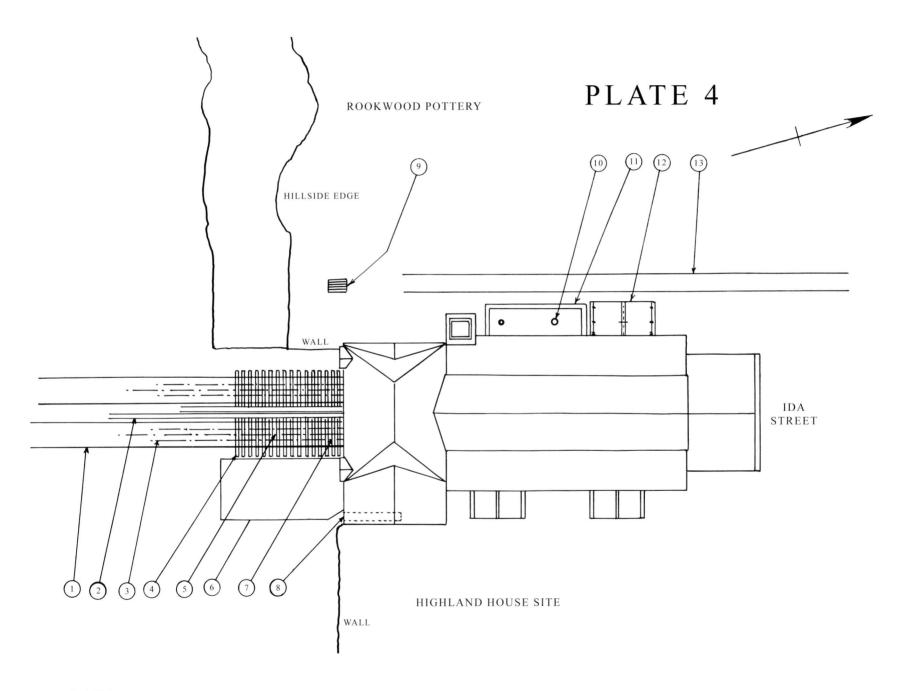

PLATE 4

ROOKWOOD POTTERY

HILLSIDE EDGE

WALL

IDA STREET

HIGHLAND HOUSE SITE

WALL

Plate 4 - Arrangement Drawing of the Top Station

A schematic view of the power-house and a partial view of the plane are shown. The figures are explained below.

1. Rail - on the plane. Weight per yard 90 lb. The plane's track gage was 7'. This seems to have been a popular gauge for inclined planes throughout the country.

2. Plank Walk - Inspectors and maintenance men used the Plank Walk (located between the two tracks).

3. Hoisting Cable - There were four of these, two per truck. They were 1-1/4" diameter, and tested to 67 tons each. They lasted 9-1/2 years.

4. Tie - Some were one piece, 24 feet long.

5. Safety Cable - 1-3/8" diameter, it lasted 7 years.

6. Repair Shed - A late addition built 1912. Various minor repair activities were carried on here. For example, the "riser wheels" (16" dia.) which kept the cable from dragging over the ties, were re-chalked, that is they were relined with wood.

7. Location of Elevating Wheels - See page 85.

8. Entrance to Engine Room - A stairway from the main floor ran to this opening. A sharp right turn led to the door of the engine room.

9. Coal Hatch - Coal bin was located under the concrete platform of which the hatch is centered.

10. Engine Exhaust Pipe

11. Water Softening Shed - Before this equipment was installed, the boilers produced three wheelbarrows of scale in a six week period.

12. Entrances to Engine Room - These three entrances were dug in the reconstruction of 1880 (possibly 1891) to permit removal of the old machinery and installation of new equipment. The other alternative would have been ripping up the main floor to gain access to the lower regions. These entrances were semi-permanently closed.

13. Coaling Track - As it appeared in last years of operation, but apparently not used since 1920's. At that time, side dump or four wheel gondolas were pulled by work cars that hauled the coal from the railroad siding.

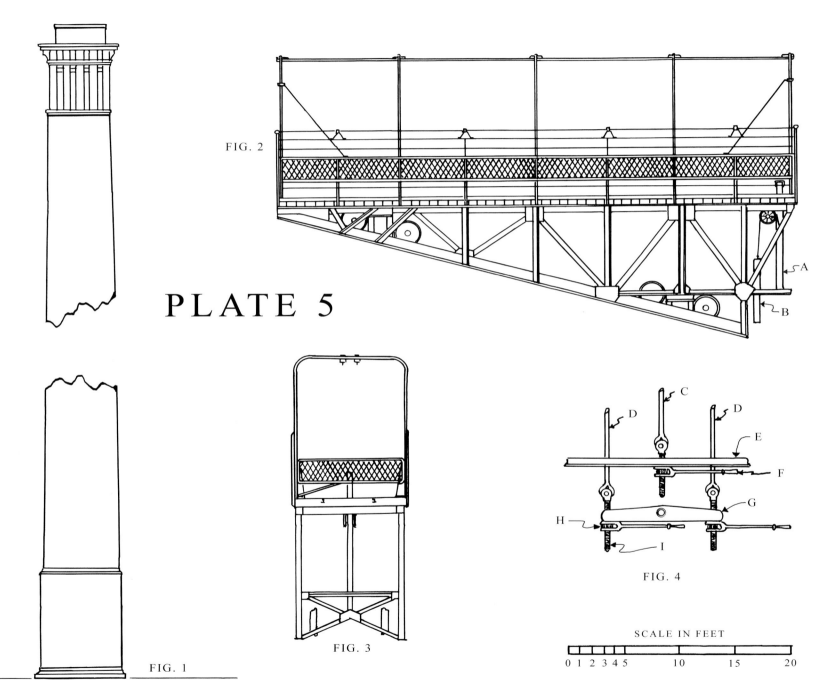

PLATE 5

FIG. 2

A

B

FIG. 1

FIG. 3

C

D

D

E

F

G

H

I

FIG. 4

SCALE IN FEET

0 1 2 3 4 5   10   15   20

Plate 5 - Truck and Chimney Details

The brick chimney or smokestack is shown in Fig. 1 of this plate. It is believed to date from the 1879/80 remodeling when the stack was moved to the west side of the building. Insurance plat maps in the collections of the Cincinnati Museum Center indicate the chimney was either 85 or 100 feet in height.

The truck or platform is shown in Figs. 2 and 3 of this plate. The drawing shows the new trucks installed in June 1936. The Lang Iron Works of Cincinnati built them of riveted steel beams and angles. The 1880 iron trucks had been lengthened in 1920 to accommodate larger eight wheel streetcars. However, after fifty-six years of hard service and exposure to the weather, the framework was so corroded that some members were eaten through by rust. The incline was shut down for three weeks while the new trucks were installed. The cables were replaced at the same time. The old wheels, axles and journal boxes were retained; however, the side frames were replaced with cast steel National type A freight car truck castings and bolsters.

Hoops were installed on the trucks to support trolley wires in about 1925. In this way, the poles could remain on the wire, even though they had no power once the truck pulled away from either station. Wire pans guided the trolley wheels through the transfer from the regular wires to the set mounted on the trucks. This arrangement saved time when loading and unloading. Formerly, wires stretched out from the top and bottom stations at just the right height over the platforms but it was necessary to pull the poles up manually to reach the wire. It should be noted that once the truck left either station, the power was off. This meant that at night the lights in the car were off as well, and so the passengers sat without the benefit of interior lighting. However, the ambient lighting from the city was fairly intense, and so, the passengers were hardly left in the dark. The absence of interior lighting in fact intensified the dramatic nighttime illumination of the city and added to the beauty of riding the incline.

The bumper stop, or the McGinty, is shown in Figs. 2 and 3 of this plate. It was made from a 4 by 9 inch steel "I" beam marked as "A" in Fig. 2. Its normal position was up or stop. The beam was held in the 'up' position by a counterweight marked as 'B' - a cable connected the counterweight to the beam. As the truck neared the bottom station, a skid placed at the tracks' center caused the counterweight to rise and the beam to drop to floor level. Hence, when the truck landed, the McGinty was down and the streetcar might pass off the truck and head for town.

Fig. 4 shows a reconstructed view of the cable connections to the underside of the truck. This apparatus was located just behind the rear wheel set. The parts are explained below:

C.   Is the center or safety cable

D.   Are the hoisting cables

E.   A beam of trucks' undercarriage

F.   Is one of the adjusting levers

G.   Is the equalizer

H.   Is one of the ratchets

I.   Is one of the adjusting screws

Photos on the following two pages depict some of these items more clearly.

Old truck near end of its service life.
Shown carrying a 2400 series street car.

Detail of old truck and it's fabricated
wheel set.

New truck as installed June 1936. Many details
visable below - cast steel truck frames; counter
weight for the McGinty; cables & a carrying
wheel in the foreground.

The steel frame of one of the new trucks is lowered into place in June 1936, near the bottom station on Lock Street. Note the broad gauge incline track.

One of the new trucks near completion at the top station. A wooden floor is being installed - rails and decking are to come.

Plate 6 - Plan and elevation of the Engine Room

Here a simplified machinery and cable layout is shown. **Fig. 1** would appear if the building and main floor were removed, leaving the engine room exposed. **Fig. 2** shows the machinery with the east wall of the foundation removed. This drawing is based on an original plan of Bert Baldwin.

The layout shown here is as the engine room appeared in its last days of operation. Nineteenth century almost to the last detail, Baldwin's design suffered no extensive alteration during its nearly 60 years of service.

The review of the machinery shall progress from left to right. The elevating wheels were mounted partially outside of the foundation. They guided the cables from the plane into the engine room. Constructed of cast iron, they were eight feet in diameter.

The balance or safety sheaves received the safety cable. The giant sheaves were twelve feet in diameter, fifteen inches wide, and were cast in sections. Four cable groves and a 5-1/2" brake drum area were turned on their circumferences. The sheaves were framed by heavy riveted steel T girders, which in turn were mounted on an inclined stone foundation. The safety sheaves were dual purpose. Balance principal was of chief importance as it was the paramount safety factor. The sheaves also served as an emergency brake. A steel band mounted with wooden brake shoes wrapped around the sheaves in a figure 8. The large lever in the center of the rig was operated by cable from the operator's cab.

The question might arise, would not one sheave serve the purposes of balancing the plane? The answer is yes and no. While balancing might be satisfied, braking would be another matter. The single sheave might effectively stop, however the cable would merely slide around it; if the hoisting cables were broken the trucks would then run wild. However, with two sheaves and the manner in which the safety cable is wrapped around them (see small diagram below safety rig) the surface area in contact with the cable is greatly multiplied. Thus, friction and braking effects are boosted making it difficult for the cable to slide. If the hoisting cables should have severed, the trucks could be stopped via the safety cable.

The threading mechanism's purpose was to lay the cable in an even single layer over the winding drums. It was a reversible screw driven by a gear, which meshed with the mortise gearing of the winding drums. (Shown in **Fig. 2** only). A few years before the abandonment, the threading machine stripped itself. The fireman called the operator who immediately stopped the plane. After some discussion, the trucks were brought to their landings with great care. A trial run proved that the threading machine was no longer of real importance, for it seems that after the long years of service, the cable had cut grooves into the wooden lagging of the winding drums. These grooves proved effective in laying out the cables.

The two winding drums were mounted on separate shafts. Each drum was fabricated from three cast iron wheels and lagged with 3-1/2" thick by 5-25/32" wide by 6' 7-1/2" long oak timbers (176 staves per drum). The diameter of the drums was 13'6". The mortise gearing at one end of each drum was fabricated from hard maple pegs (15'16" dia.). The shaft averaged 12" in diameter and was 22' long. The brake bands were 6-1/2" wide and with the safety brakes, were steel bands with hard maple shoes. They were the regular service brakes.

Single acting brakes were originally installed. Thus only the brake on the descending truck was effective. With the installation of the Lilly control (see "Safety") it was decided to install double acting brakes and yet depend on the existing pedal and lever arrangement for setting. The trial run proved to be a near disaster. The trucks had to be stopped by reversing the winding engines.

While the double acting brake could operate no matter what the direction of rotation, they required a great deal more force than the old single acting brake. Obviously, the operator was limited as to the amount of force he could apply to the brake pedal. The double acting brakes were kept, but an equalizing arrangement was instituted whereby both bands were set at once.

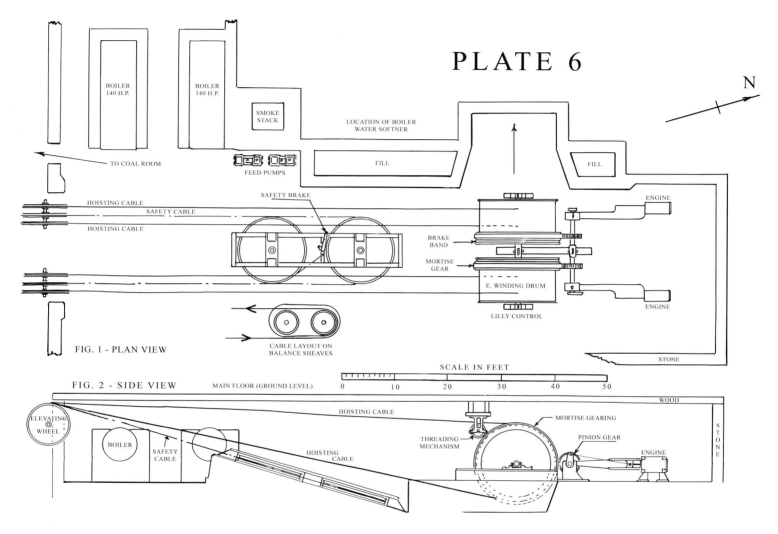

PLATE 6

N

BOILER 140 H.P.

BOILER 140 H.P.

SMOKE STACK

LOCATION OF BOILER WATER SOFTNER

TO COAL ROOM

FEED PUMPS

FILL

FILL

HOISTING CABLE

SAFETY CABLE

HOISTING CABLE

SAFETY BRAKE

ENGINE

BRAKE BAND

MORTISE GEAR

E. WINDING DRUM

LILLY CONTROL

ENGINE

STONE

FIG. 1 - PLAN VIEW

CABLE LAYOUT ON BALANCE SHEAVES

SCALE IN FEET

0   10   20   30   40   50

FIG. 2 - SIDE VIEW

MAIN FLOOR (GROUND LEVEL)

WOOD

ELEVATING WHEEL

BOILER

SAFETY CABLE

HOISTING CABLE

HOISTING CABLE

THREADING MECHANISM

MORTISE GEARING

PINION GEAR

ENGINE

STONE

The pinion gears, which drove the mortise gears of the drums, were mounted on the crankshaft of the engines. They were cast iron (or steel) 19-1/2" wide and about 4' in diameter. In the last years of operation they showed greater wear than the wooden mortise gearing. They were operated "dry".

The steam engines were 20" x 36" non-releasing Corliss's built by Lane and Bodley Company of this city. The cranks were "quartered" (set at 90 degrees, a common practice on steam locomotives) so that the engines would not hit dead center simultaneously. These were large engines as shown in photograph page 81.

The boilers sat off to one side of the engine room in a low chamber with a vaulted brick ceiling. The boilers operated at 125 P.S.I. The feedwater pumpers were made locally by the John H. McGowan Company on Central Avenue.

Plate 7 - The Bottom Station

Data for this drawing was gathered while the original building remained standing on Lock Street in 1963. The structure was not demolished until 1974 to make way for approaches to the I-471 Bridge. The structure is believed to be the second bottom station erected on the site. The original 1876 station was designed for the fixed cab style of incline operation where passengers boarded and exited the small horse car-like vehicles that traveled up and down the plane for its first four years of its existence (see p. 76, top left). When the open truck style of operation was introduced, a new bottom station was required, for now only foot passengers boarded at this point. Hence, a much smaller depot would suffice. It served as many things: a ticket office, waiting room, shelter for employees who worked the gates and bell signals, agents who collected or sold tickets as well as answering the repetitive questions that travelers are wont to ask. The little brick building had a large pair of doors topped by a fanlight, a tin hip roof and a heavy entablature that spanned over the incline tracks. It bore the letters "Eden Park Railway".

When the line was electrified in 1890, more overhead clearance was needed for the trolley wires and so the entablature was removed. At the same time, the main door was converted into a window. The corner of the building was cut off at an angle for a new front door and a flat roof replaced the hip roof. The interior was finished with stamped tin walls and ceiling in place of plaster. The odd little building remained in this shape until it was pulled down.

Second bottom station as it appeared in about 1885 when horse cars were in use. The building was remodeled in 1890 for electric street cars. This view is from a contemporary post card.

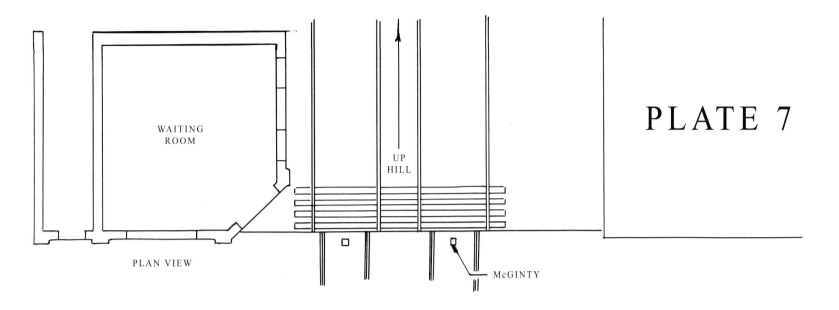

WAITING
ROOM

PLAN VIEW

UP
HILL

McGINTY

PLATE 7

LOCK STREET

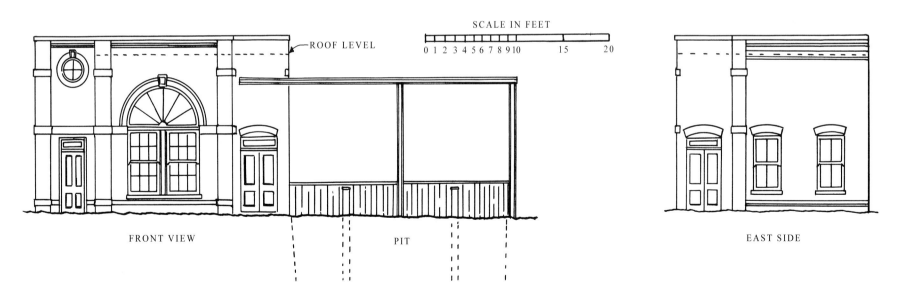

ROOF LEVEL

SCALE IN FEET

0 1 2 3 4 5 6 7 8 9 10   15   20

FRONT VIEW

PIT

EAST SIDE

The bottom station on Lock Street (near Fifth Street) as it appeared in it's last years, roughly 1890 to 1948.

Plate 8 - The Incline Plane Side Elevation
(See foldout in pocket at the end of this volume)

On first viewing of this drawing, most observers are convinced it is all-wrong, surely it was steeper than what is shown here. Why, I remember riding it and it was almost straight down. In front-on photographs, the incline also appears to run down hill on an acute angle, yet in truth, it ran at just 29.4 degrees. When drawn out full length, it appears deceptively gentle.

The drawing reproduced here was copied from a series of small-scale plans produced in 1914 for the Cincinnati Traction Company. I made copies from the originals, then in files of the Cincinnati Street Railway at their Winton Shops in about 1955. When pieced together, the series produce a picture of the hillside trestlework. There were 53 bents starting with number one at the bottom of the grade. Actually, the first 200 feet ran in a shallow cut and was graded and ballasted like a regular railroad track. The masonry portion of the bents looked like poured concrete monoliths with straight and uniform surfaces. They were, in fact, built-up from stone recovered from hillside quarries on the slopes of Mt. Adams and in real life presented a far more rustic appearance than our drawings suggest. The upright wooden members of the bents were 14 by 14-inch timbers. The cross bracing was made from 5 by 9 and 5 by 10 inch timbers. The design appears rather haphazard and while the structure sustained its load for several decades without failure, the structure was found leaning uphill during its last years of operation. We might expect it to sag in opposite directions considering the natural forces of gravity. Just how much science was involved in the design is a matter of speculation but modern engineers were eager to redo the entire arrangement following an inspection made in 1949.

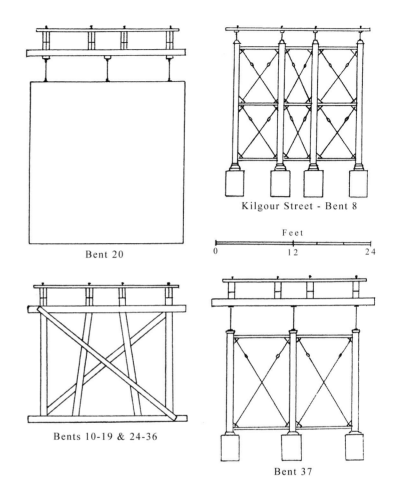

Kilgour Street - Bent 8

Bent 20

Feet

0   12   24

Bents 10-19 & 24-36

Bent 37

The quantity of wood in the old structure was enormous. Just the crossties equaled 29,696 board feet of lumber. It should be noted that most of the ties consisted of 4 inch by 8 inch by 11-foot timbers. But over 200 of the ties were 23 feet long. The footpath at the center of the plane was made from two 1" x 12" wide boards. Small wood strips were nailed across to offer a more secure foothold. Steel "T" rails, ninety pounds to the yard, completed the 7-foot gauge track.

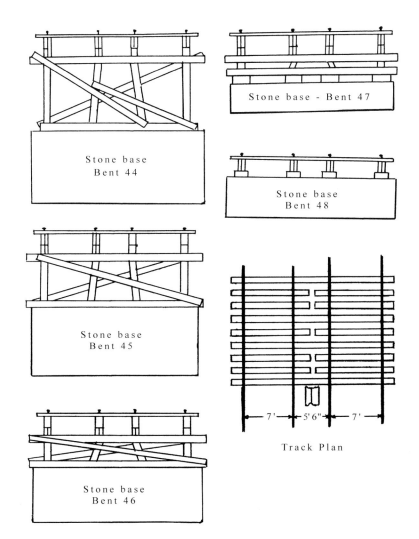

Stone base - Bent 47

Stone base
Bent 44

Stone base
Bent 48

Stone base
Bent 45

|←— 7' —→|←5'6"→|←— 7' —→|

Track Plan

Stone base
Bent 46

Truck and streetcar crossing over Oregon St. about 1940.

The hillside trestle crossed three minor city streets. These were residential in nature but did carry some traffic and so must be crossed over in a manner that would not limit passage. Iron bridges were erected in 1876 to cross over Kilgour, Baum and Oregon Streets. The smallest of these structures passed over Kilgour Street and, from its antique design, may date back to the original bridge (see pg 108).

The uprights were called Phoenix Columns. These cylindrical rolled wrought iron columns were fabricated from four flanged sections riveted together. They were 8 inches in diameter and 12 inches wide over the flange. Samuel J. Reeves of the Phoenix Bridge Works, Phoenixville, PA, introduced the design in 1862. The two other bridges were made from fabricated iron or steel plate girders. The date of these bridges is uncertain but they most likely were installed during the 1890-91 reconstruction. In so many instances, we must plead ignorance because of the absence of original records. At the same time, conflicting evidence found in

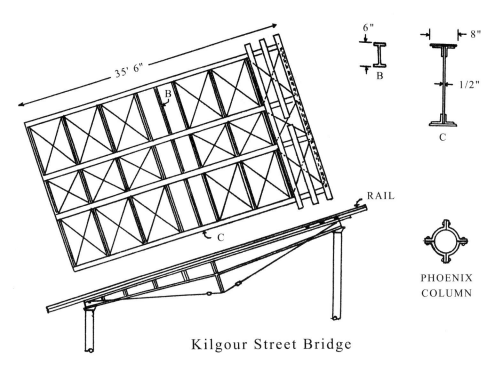

Kilgour Street Bridge

secondary sources adds to the frustration of those attempting to reconstruct the incline's true history. The old saying that figures lie and liars figure, is all too often confirmed as we dig for reliable information. The length of the plane is a case in point. The Ohio Railroad Commission 1880 Report gives the length as 1000 feet. In their 1883 report, they cite 974 feet. The October 10, 1895 issue of *Engineering News* claims a length of 945 feet. *Cassier's Magazine* was another respected technical journal. In its issue for June 1897, it claimed the Mt. Adams inclined plane was 999 feet long. The Cincinnati Street Railway's "Dope Book" agrees with the *Engineering News* figures. The 'Dope Book' was a small notebook kept by Miss Caroline Hein as a quick reference for factual matter concerning the transit companies properties and operations. When an inquirer called, everyone knew to look it up in the 'Dope Book'. However, the veracity of this handy little volume might be in question since sources were rarely included.

View of the lower end of the Kilgour St. Bridge and related Phoenix columns.

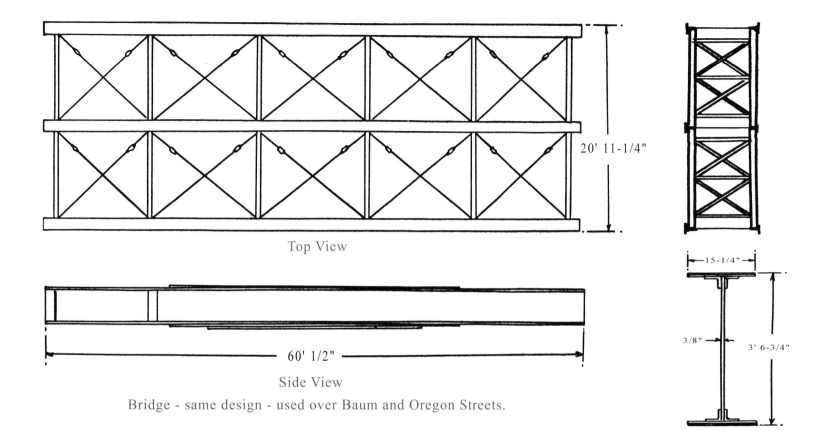

Top View

Side View

Bridge - same design - used over Baum and Oregon Streets.

The researcher of today is left to wonder who was right about the dimensions? Perhaps none of them. Perhaps all of them. It would depend very much on who was measuring and from where to where they placed their tapes. Perhaps the numbers were carelessly recorded or inaccurately transcribed by a typist or typesetter. Maybe it was just sloppy math but whatever might explain this 55-foot variance, we can be certain that good old reliable human error was involved.

In closing our remarks on Plate 8, we must take note of the hundreds of small pulley wheels placed along the length of the plane. The wheels were placed in sets of three, about every twenty feet. They were only about 16 inches in diameter but they performed a useful service. It was their job to carry the cables and keep them from dragging along the cross ties. Dragging cable would cut into the ties and wear them out in the process. These little sheaves could be set whirling by the passing cables and so lubricating their bearings was one of the tasks of the trackmen. The pulleys had a wooden lining to lessen wear of the cable as they passed over the sheaves.

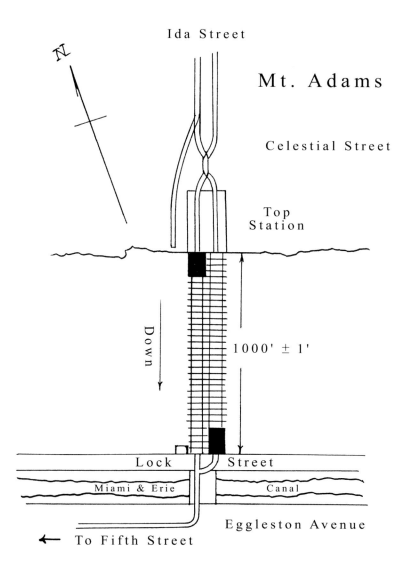

Ida Street

Mt. Adams

Celestial Street

Top
Station

Down

1000' ± 1'

Lock   Street

Miami & Erie   Canal

Eggleston Avenue

← To Fifth Street

Track plan of the Mt. Adams Incline, drawn by the author.
(Not to scale.)

Summary of Report on Electrification of Mt. Adams Incline - October 25, 1932
J. A. Noertker [*] - W. J. Lewis

The Price Hill Incline had been electrified four years before this report was written. Great economies had been experienced from this operation; most of the Pittsburgh planes electrified about this time. Therefore, it would seem quite plausible for the Street Railway to investigate such a conversion, considering it would pay for itself in less than five years. The following is an introduction to the report, addressed to Harley L. Swift, Assist. General Manager of the Cincinnati Street Railway:

"Herewith is the report on the Electrification of Mt. Adams Incline that you requested some time ago. The report shows that it is possible to effect an annual savings of at least $13,000 in the cost of labor required to operate the Mt. Adams Incline by making a new capital investment of $55,000.

There are many who decry projects of this type at times when a great surplus of labor exists and there are many who approve of this type of project so that a greater number of men may be put to work in the immediate present, hoping that within a few years something will happen to increase the demand for the retired labor. From a practical point of view, however, it seems to me that where a project such as the Mt. Adams Incline rendering a definite service to the public is in danger of being abandoned on account of excessive operating cost, it is the part of common sense to reduce these costs to a minimum.

There are strong sentimental and civic reasons in favor

[*] Joseph. A. Noertker was a member of the C.S.R. engineering staff starting in 1923. He was a native Cincinnatian and a graduate of the U.C. Engineering School. He retired in 1967 and died May 23, 1988.

of continuing the operation of the plane and we do not think they can or should be disregarded. However, we believe it would go a long way toward the solution of this problem to consider the operation of the plane from a transportation viewpoint. It is our opinion therefore that a transportation survey of Mt. Adams would be of great value in determining the action that should be taken."

Mr. Noertker praised the operation of steam equipment, …"acceleration is smooth and landings are made neatly and with practically no impact. It is improbable that electrification could improve operation. As a matter of fact, unless electrification equipment is selected with a great deal of care, it is probable that the operation will not be as good."

The economies would be realized almost totally from a reduction in employees. It was calculated that work force would be halved, resulting in an estimated savings of $13,000 a year. Of course, the employees to be eliminated would be the fireman and stationary steam engineers. According to estimates, electrical power would cost more than coal.

New winding machinery was to be installed, but the old safety rig would be retained. Total estimated cost of new machinery and its installation was estimated at $54,868. The report revealed much information not directly related to the electrification project. Under appendix "A" reports of revenue were listed from 1929 to the first six months of 1932. Revenue for hauling freight dropped from $1065.25 (1929) to $279.60 (1932). Foot passenger revenues held up quite well, however; $6, 777.65 (1929) to $5,173.63 (1932).

Appendix 'A' further stated that a 'Jerky' motor coach operated over Route 49 Zoo-Eden from December 1930 to January 1931.

Needless to say, the electrification was not carried out. Inability or reluctance of the Street Railway to expend the necessary capital during the depression; uncertainties of continued operation; difficulty of obtaining new equipment during the war, are the probable reasons the plan was not executed. How unwise this was is a matter of speculation. It seems that with the electrification, the plane might have continued to operate. Quite probably there were other considerations not now apparent on why the electrification project was not executed.

Incline foot passenger near the end of operation.
Good detail view of truck gate.

Summary - Hanley and Young Report March 1, 1949

Messrs. Hanley and Young, Engineers of Cincinnati, made a survey of Mt. Adams Incline plane and power station building. They concluded "that a resumption of operations would be hazardous."

The planes' trestlework was a particular concern. There was a fundamental lack in its design. The structure was capable of supporting the weight of the trucks; however, no consideration was given to"longitudinal forces" (tension or lateral pulling effect of the cables). The result was that the structure was literally being pulled up the hill. The stone piers and bents[1] were leaning uphill. The piers themselves were decadent - "almost all of them show heavy cracking and swelling, and the interior mortar…has broken down into sand." As already mentioned, they were badly out of plumb.

The Kilgour Street Bridge was in fair condition; however, the Baum and Oregon Street Bridges were dangerous. "They have slid on their piers…, bracing members have in most cases sheared away their connection,…the metal has been seriously attacked by rust." The wooden plane could be rebuilt, with anchorage provisions for longitudinal forces, for about $100,000. Estimates for building of an entirely new steel structure were given. Steel plane would cost only $3500 more than rebuilding wooden structure. Cost of maintenance would be reduced by several thousand dollars per year.

Bent 40 showing effect of lateral forces on the trestle.

Bent 9 and the upper Phoenix columns from the Kilgour Street Bridge.

[1] Bents are vertical supports - members of the trestle.

The prospect of rebuilding or building a new plane presented a dangerous and expensive operation. "The right of way is very narrow (approximately 25 feet) and the adjoining property is largely occupied, which, with the grade of the hill, will make it necessary to do much of the work without the benefit of heavy equipment, and the cost of handling material in and out will also tend to be high. These factors are reflected in the estimated prices."

Lower bridge pier for the Baum St. Bridge. The pier is out of plumb due to a crumbling interior.

The power-house was in comparatively good condition. A new roof was needed, as might be a new floor if the city insisted on conformance to its fire law regulations. The concrete deck on the west side of the building, also roof of boiler room was in need of attention. Since heavy coal trucks passed over this, it would have to be rebuilt if steam operations were to continue. [2]

In a letter dated March 2, 1949, Mr. Young advised the company that if a fire-proof floor were installed, the power-house building might well be removed for the floor would be waterproof. Destruction of the top station was not favored by the preservationists.

[2] Consideration of electrification was again very much in vogue.

View looking down the Incline Plane trestle. Warped and failing trestle pieces and the narrow right-of-way are apparent.

View of west side of the Highland House and the Ida Street entrance to the top station of the Mt. Adams Incline. Note the headlight hanging just beneath the Eden Park Railway sign on the station. This illuminated Ida Street for night streetcar operation. Photo 1880c.

114

Timeline

Cincinnati Street Railways

1845   Omnibus operations begin in Cincinnati.

1859   97 omnibus licenses issued to operate in the city.

1859   September 14, the first horse cars begin service on the "Blue" or Seventh Street Line.

1859-60   More horse car lines open by the John Street, Third Street and the East End Line.

1867   Route 8 reaches Mt. Auburn.

1872   The Main Street Incline opens.

1873   Five lines merge as the Cincinnati Consolidated Railway.

1875   The Cincinnati Horse car system has 14 routes, 45 miles of track, 1000 horses, 550 employees and 165 cars.

1875   The Price Hill Incline is opened.

1876   The Mt. Adams and Clifton Inclines open.

1880   The Cincinnati Street Railway is organized to operate ten lines.

1881-1882   The city has 18 car lines, about 60 miles of track, 203 cars and 995 horses.

1885   The city has four separate transit companies: C.S.R. operates 75.5 miles, 2000 horses, 255 cars; Mt. A & E. P. operates 16 miles, 320 horses, 40 cars; C.I.P. operates 6 miles, 150 horses, 25 cars; Columbia Dummy Line operates 5 miles with 9 cars.

1885   July 17 - The city's first cable car line is opened by the Mt. A. & E. P. on Gilbert Avenue. By 1888 the line is extended to Blair Avenue.

1886   September 25 - The first section of the Vine Street cable line is opened by the Cincinnati Street Railway. In 1888 the second section was opened into Clifton.

1887   July - Mail service begins on Gilbert Avenue cable line.

1889   October 15 - Accident on Main Street Incline kills 6 passengers.

1890   Cincinnati Street Railways are carrying approximately 37 million passengers per year. U. S. Census says 37,905,370.

Timeline (cont.)

1890   The five operating companies owned 2163 horses and 539 cars. Most lines are being converted to electric operations.

1891   The city has a total of 67.9 route miles (148 track miles) of street railways of which 49.5 are horse powered, 5.8 are electric and 12.5 are cable. About 80% of system is controlled by the C.S.R. The system had grown 40% since 1880.

1895   Electric lines reach out to Westwood and College Hill. The city has 217 miles of track, 1155 cars and only five horse cars remain in service.

1896   Mt. Auburn Cable Line is sold to Cincinnati Street Railway. A new repair shop is opened on Spring Grove Avenue near Chester Park. It is later re-organized into the Cincinnati Car Company.

1898   Both the Gilbert Avenue and Vine Street Cable Lines are converted to electric traction.

1898   The Main Street Incline is closed.

1901   The C.S.R. system is leased to the Cincinnati Traction Co. on February 21 and became part of the Widener-Elkins Traction Empire.

1902   The system carries 94.2 million passengers. The Mt. Auburn Cable is converted to electric traction. Eight wheel cars enter service. These larger vehicles will soon replace the smaller 4 wheel cars.

1909   A street railway electric power plant is built at Pendleton.

1911   The traction company transports 97.7 million passengers.

1912   The system has 222 miles of track and 1364 cars.

1913   A major labor upheaval takes place as conductors and motormen go on strike.

1913   March - George B. Kerper, former President of the Mt. A. & E. P. Railway, dies. He is 74 years of age.

1914   October 30 - John Kilgour long time mogul in local transit affairs dies. He was active in banking, telephones and the wholesale grocery trade, as well as city transit.

1920   Work starts on subway - stops about 1927.

1922-1923   2400 series cars are delivered.

1923   10 cent fare begins.

1923   December - Crosstown Line begins operation.

Timeline (cont.)

1924	Single truck cars are retired.
1925	November 1 - Traction Co. lease ends. C.S.R. resumes operations with Walter A. Draper as President.
1926	Motor Bus operations begin by C.S.R.
1928	100 series cars enter service; Winton Shops opens - now buys electricity from C. G. & E.
1930	Cinti, Lawrenceburg & Aurora interurban is abandoned.
1935	Cinti, Georgetown & Portsmouth is abandoned.
1936	Cinti, Milford & Loveland interurban is abandoned.
1939	Test P.C.C. cars begins.
1939	Last section of the Cincinnati & Lake Erie is abandoned.
1946	Local transit ridership peaks at 132 million but falls into a rapid decline as WWII emergency ends.
1951	April 29 - End street car service.
1973	August - Metro takes over from Cincinnati Transit.

From the *Cincinnati Commercial*, July 5, 1886.

Bibliography

For more information we recommend the following list of books and pamphlets. This listing may not be complete, but it contains the core of the available literature on the subject.

Condit, Carl W. — The Railroad and the City Technological and Urbanistic History of Cincinnati. Columbus, 1977.

Espy, Arthur — Code of Franchises Cincinnati, 1914. Covers street railways.

Fairchild, C.B. — Street Railways, Their Construction, Operation and Maintenance New York, 1892.

Hilton, George W. — The Cable Car in America Berkley, 1971

Keenan, Jack — The Cincinnati and Lake Erie Railway. San Marino, CA, 1975.

Lehmann, Terry W. and Clark, Earl W. Jr. — The Green Line: The Cincinnati, Newport and Covington Railway. Chicago, 2001

McNeil, David — Railroad with Three Gauges, The Cincinnati, Georgetown, & Portsmouth RR. Cincinnati, 1986.

Cincinnati and Columbus Traction Company Cincinnati, 1996

Life Along the Trolley Line Cincinnati, 1989

Middleton, William D. — The Time of the Trolley Milwaukee, 1967.

Miller, John A. — Fares Please New York, 1941.

Smalley, Stephen B. — Cincinnati, Georgetown, and Portsmouth. Cincinnati, 1972 & 1973 - two booklets.

Interurban Railway and Terminal: Black Line Cincinnati, 1972

Wagner, Richard M. — Curved-Side Cars Built by the Cincinnati Car Company. Cincinnati, 1965.

Wagner, Richard M, and Roy J. Wright — Cincinnati Street Cars. A series of booklets published by the authors between 1968 and 1985. A final volume, No. 10, appeared in 1997 with Tom McNamara as author/compiler.

White, John H. Jr.

Chapter 1 — "From Top to Bottom: Cincinnati's Inclines and Hilltop Houses" Timeline, (Ohio Historical Society) Jan/Feb 1995, pp. 26-39.

Chapter 2 — "The Cincinnati Inclined Plane Railway Company: The Mount Auburn Incline and Lookout House," Bulletin , Cincinnati Historical Society, April 1967, pp 93-107.

Chapter 3 — "The Mt. Adams and Eden Park Inclined Railway," Bulletin, the Historical and Philosophical Society of Ohio, October 1959, pp. 242-276.

Chapter 4 — "The Mt. Adams Incline: It's History, Operation, and Untimely End." No previous publication of this account.

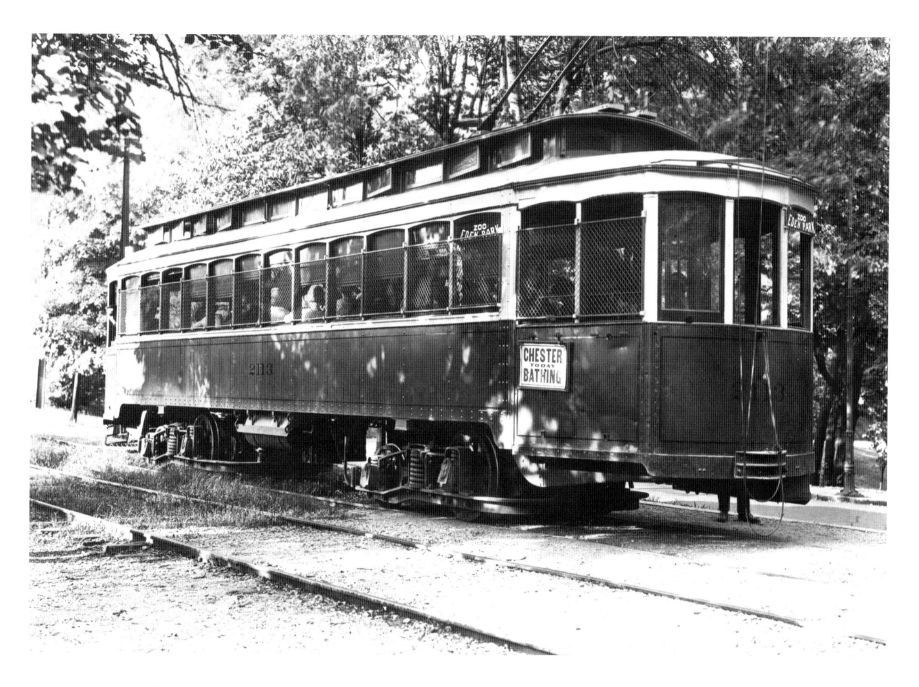

Zoo-Eden Park car outside the Art Museum, July 20, 1926. N.A. Berthol photo from the authors' collection.

Index

Aussicht auf Mount Adams von einem Kirchthurm.

View of Mt. Adams past the steeple of First Presbyterian Church, Fourth & Main Streets from German text book 'Cincinnati in Wort and Bild', 1888. The smoke is from the Mt. Adams Incline power house. The Ida Street bridge is clearly visable left of the Incline.

121

Contemporary illustration of Fifth and Walnut Streets showing cable, electric and horse-drawn street cars in service simultaniously. *Street Railway Journal*, March 1892, pg 127.

What a difference 60 years can make. Both photos are the Mt. Adams Incline taken near either end of it's service life. The photo on the left shows the incline in 1876, as first built.. The photo on the right, taken in 1936, shows many of the changes to the Incline, and Mt. Adams, during those years.

"Step Forward! Please,"

Gilbert Avenue Cable Car circa 1890's from the booklet *Suburban Homes* issued by the Baltimore & Ohio Southwestern Railroad.